KABBALAH CENTRE BOOKS

The Zohar *24 volumes by Rabbi Shimon bar Yohai, The cardinal work in the literature of Kabbalah - original Aramaic text with Hebrew translation and commentary by Rabbi Yehudah Ashlag.*

Miracles, Mysteries and Prayer Vol. I, II, Rabbi Philip S. Berg (also available in French and Spanish)

Kabbalah for the Layman Vol. I,Rabbi Philip S. Berg (also available in Hebrew, Spanish, French, Russian, Italian, German, Persian, Chinese and Portuguese)

Kabbalah for the Layman Vol. III, Rabbi Philip S. Berg (also available in Hebrew, Spanish, French and Italian)

Reincarnation: Wheels of a Soul Rabbi Phili S. Berg (also available in Hebrew, Spanish, French, Italian, Russian and Persian)

Astrology: The Star Connection Rabbi Philip S. Berg (also available in Hebrew, Spanish, French and Italian)

Time Zones: Creating Order from Chaos Rabbi Philip S. Berg (also available in French, Spanish, Hebrew and Persian)

To The Power of One Rabbi Philip S. Berg (also available in Spanish and French)

Power of the Aleph Beth Vol. I, II, Rabbi Philip S. Berg (also available in Hebrew, French and Spanish)

The Kabbalah Connection Rabbi Philip S. Berg (also available in Spanish)

Gift of the Bible Rabbi Yehuda Ashlag / Foreword by Rabbi Philip S. Berg (also available in Hebrew, French and Spanish)

Zohar: Parashat Pinhas Vol. I, II, III, Translated compiled and edited by Rabbi Philip S. Berg (also available in Spanish)

An Entrance to the Tree of Life Compiled and edited by Rabbi Philip S. Berg (also available in Spanish)

Ten Luminous Emanations Vol. I, II, III, Compiled and edited by Rabbi Philip S. Berg (also available in Hebrew)

An Entrance to The Zohar Compiled and edited by Rabbi Philip S. Berg

General Principles of Kabbalah Rabbi M. Luzzatto (also available in Italian)

Light of Redemption by Rabbi Levi Krakovsky

SOON TO BE PUBLISHED

Ten Luminous Emanations Vol. III, IV compiled and edited by Rabbi Philip S. Berg

Time Zones: Creating Order from Chaos Rabbi Philip S. Berg, Russian Translation

To The Power of One Rabbi Philip S. Berg Russian and Hebrew Translations

BOOKS AND TAPES AVAILABLE
AT BOOKSELLERS AND KABBALAH CENTRES AROUND THE WORLD.

KABBALAH
FOR THE
LAYMAN

VOLUME TWO

KABBALAH

KABBALAH
FOR THE
LAYMAN

VOLUME TWO

RABBI PHILIP S. BERG

FIRST EDITION
November 1988

SECOND EDITION
November 1993

ISBN 0-943688-82-5 (Hard cover)
0-943688-83-3 (Soft cover)

For further information:

THE RESEARCH CENTRE OF KABBALAH
85-03 114th Street, Richmond Hill
NEW YORK 11418

-or--

P.O.BOX 14168
THE OLD CITY, JERUSALEM

PRINTED IN U.S.A.
1993

*To the spiritual fulfillment
of my family*

Parents: Nathan and Klara
Brothers: Ben Zion and Eliezer
Sisters: Ethel and Lilian

*And through them
to the world
and through them
to the universe*

From

David Lester

For my wife

KAREN

In the vastness of cosmic space
and the infinity of lifetimes,
it is my bliss to share
a soulmate and
an age of Aquarius
with you.

TABLE OF CONTENTS

ABOUT THE CENTRES

Kabbalah is mystical Judaism. It is the deepest and most hidden meaning of the *Torah*, or Bible. Through the ultimate knowledge and mystical practices of Kabbalah, one can reach the highest spiritual levels attainable. Although many people rely on belief, faith, and dogmas in pursuing the meaning of life, the unknown, and the unseen, Kabbalists seek a spiritual connection with the Creator and the forces of the Creator, so that the strange becomes familiar, and faith becomes knowledge.

Throughout history, those who knew and practiced the Kabbalah were extremely careful in their dissemination of the knowledge for they knew the masses of mankind had not yet prepared for the ultimate truth of existence. Today Kabbalists know, through Kabbalistic knowledge, that it is not only proper but necessary to make available the Kabbalah to all who seek it

The Research Centre of Kabbalah is an independent, non- profit institute founded in Israel in 1922. The Centre provides research, information, and assistance to those who seek the insights of Kabbalah. The Centre offers public lectures, classes, seminars, and excursions to mystical sites at branches in Israel in Jerusalem, Tel Aviv, Haifa, Beer Sheva, Ashdod, and Ashkelon— and in the United States in New York and los Angeles. Branches have been opened in Mexico, Montreal, Toronto, Paris, Hong Kong and Taiwan. Thousands of people have benefited by the Centre's activities, and the Centre's publishing of Kabbalistic material continues to be the most comprehensive of its kind in the world including translations in English, Hebrew, Russian, German, Portuguese, French, Spanish, Farsi (Persian) and Chinese

Kabbalah can provide one with the true meaning of their being and the knowledge necessary for their ultimate benefit. It can show one spirituality which is beyond belief. The Research Centre of Kabbalah will continue to make available the Kabbalah to all those who seek it.

ABOUT THE ZOHAR

The ZOHAR, the basic source of the Kabbalah was written by Rabbi Shimon bar Yohai while hiding from the Romans in a cave in Pe'quin for 13 years. It was later brought to light by Rabbi Moses de Leon in Spain and further revealed through the Safed Kabbalists and the Lurianic system of Kabbalah.

The programs of the Research Centre of Kabbalah have been established to provide opportunities for learning, teaching, research, and demonstration of specialized knowledge drawn from the ageless wisdom of the Zohar and the Jewish sages. Long kept from the masses, today this knowledge should be shared by all who seek to understand the deeper meaning of our Jewish heritage, a more profound meaning of life. Modern science is only beginning to discover what our sages veiled in symbolism. This knowledge is of a very practical nature and can be applied daily for the betterment of our lives and of mankind.

Our courses and materials deal with the zoharic understanding of each weekly portion of the Torah. Every facet of Jewish life is covered and other dimensions, hitherto unknown, provide a deeper connection to a superior Reality. Three important beginning courses cover such aspects as: Time, Space and Motion; Reincarnation, Marriage, Divorce, Kabbalistic Meditation, Limitation of the five senses, Illusion-Reality, Four Phases, Male and Female, Death, Sleep, Dreams, Food: what is kosher and why; Circumcision, Redemption of the First Born, Shatnes, Shabbat.

Darkness cannot prevail in the presence of Light. A darkened room must respond even to the lighting of a candle. As we share this moment together we are beginning to witness, and indeed some of us are already participating in a people's revolution of enlightenment The darkened clouds of strife and conflict will make their presence felt only as long as the Eternal Light remains concealed.

The Zohar now remains a final, if not the only, solution to infusing the cosmos with the revealed Light of the Force. The Zohar is not a book about religion. Rather, the Zohar is concerned with the relationship between the unseen forces of the cosmos, the Force, and the impact on Man.

The Zohar promises that with the ushering in of the Age of Aquarius the cosmos will become readily accessible to human understanding. It states that in the days of the Messiah "there will no longer be the necessity for one to request of his neighbor, teach me wisdom" (Zohar III, p58a). "One day they will no longer teach every man his neighbor and every man his brother, saying know the Lord. For they shall all know Me, from the youngest to the oldest of them (Jeremiah 31:34).

We can and must regain control of our lives and environment. To achieve this objective the Zohar provides us with an opportunity to transcend the crushing weight of universal negativity

The daily perusing of the Zohar, without any attempt at translation or "understanding" will fill our consciousness with the Light, improving our well-being and influencing all in our environment toward positive attitudes. Even the scanning of the Zohar by those unfamiliar with the Hebrew Aleph Beth will accomplish the same result.

The connection that we establish through scanning the Zohar is a connection and unity with the Light of the Lord. The letters, even if we do not consciously know Hebrew or Aramaic, are the channels through which the connection is made and could be likened to dialing the right telephone number, or typing in the right codes to run a computer program. The connection is established at the metaphysical level of our being and radiates into our physical plane of existence...but first there is the metaphysical "fixing". We have to consciously, through positive thoughts and actions, permit the immense power of the Zohar to radiate love, harmony and peace into our lives for us to share with all humanity and the universe.

As we enter the years ahead, the Zohar will continue to be a people's book, striking a sympathetic chord in the hearts and minds of those who long for peace, truth and relief from suffering. In the face of crises and catastrophe it has the ability to resolve agonizing human afflictions by restoring each individual's relationship with the Force.

ABOUT THE AUTHOR

RABBI PHILIP S. BERG is Dean of the Research Centre of Kabbalah. Born in New York City, into a family descended from a long line of Rabbis, he is an ordained Orthodox Rabbi (from the renowned rabbinical seminary Torat VaDaat). While traveling to Israel in 1962, he met his Kabbalistic master, Rabbi Yehudah Zvi Brandwein, student of Rabbi Yehudah Ashlag Z"L and then Dean of the Research Centre of Kabbalah. During that period the Centre expanded substantially with the establishment of the United States branch in 1965 through which it currently disseminates and distributes its publications. Rabbi Berg did research at the Centre under the auspices of his beloved teacher Rabbi Brandwein Z"L, writing books on such topics as the origins of Kabbalah, creation, cosmic consciousness, energy, and the myths of the speed of light and the light barrier. Following the death of his master in 1969, Rabbi Berg assumed the position of Dean of the Centre, expanding its publication program through the translation of source material on the Kabbalah into English and other languages. Rabbi Berg moved with his devoted and dedicated wife Karen to Israel in 1971, where they opened the doors of the Centre to *all* seekers of self identity, establishing centres in all major cities throughout Israel, while at the same time lecturing at the City University of Tel Aviv. They returned to the United States in 1981 to further establish centres of learning in major cities all over the world. In addition to publishing scientific and popular articles, Rabbi Berg is the author, translator and/or editor of eighteen other books, including the *Kabbalah for the Layman* series, *Wheels of a Soul,* and *Time Zones.*

ACKNOWLEDGEMENT

I would like to express my gratitude to Robert L. Fisher for compiling and editing the manuscript.

Rabbi Philip S. Berg
New York, November, 1987

PREFACE

NEGLECTED, MALIGNED AND TRIVIALIZED,
KABBALAH endures. Despite voluminous "empirical scientific
evidence" to the contrary, contemporary man clings tenaciously to
arcane traditions and ancient supernatural beliefs. In this age of
technological wonders, all manner of spiritual and metaphysical
doctrines and practices still thrive and flourish.

There has to be a reason. Physicists, those bastions of
rationality, are by no means impervious to the magnetism of metaphysics. Einstein credited Intuition as the principal factor in his
discovery of the theory of Relativity. He spent his remaining years
searching for a simple, elegant formula by which to explain the
nature of the universe within the framework of a single unified
conceptual construct. Subsequent generations of scientists have
taken up the gauntlet and the search for a "GUT" or Grand
Unified Theory continues to this day.

Is Physics only now learning what Metaphysics has known all along? For anyone who has entered the sanctuary of Kabbalah the answer can only be emphatic in the affirmative. In these fast-paced and fragmented times, bombarded as we are by sensory stimuli, what perfect pleasure it gives one to enter the refuge of an ancient tradition that is at the same time so elemental and yet 50 complete. Here, where the mighty cult of progress holds no sway, we find a life affirming doctrine that transcends the intellect without denying the Mind.

It is with eager anticipation that kabbalists await scientific verification of a Grand Unified Theory, for not only will that announcement corroborate many metaphysical philosophies and doctrines, it will confirm what kabbalists have known for centuries, namely, that there is another invisible, all-pervading energy-intelligence, not unlike gravity or electromagnetism, that has yet to be scientifically substantiated, and that every phase, every facet of this primal force field is in constant instantaneous communication with every other phase and facet. Ironically, with the establishment of the Grand Unified Theory, science will be forced to accept and once again embrace those very selfsame spiritual, supernal, and supernatural doctrines and traditions that it struggled so arduously to discredit and destroy.

In fact, Kabbalah and Science may have more in common than practitioners of either discipline would care to admit. Both, after all, seek to explain the true nature of existence. Far from being a mere escapist panacea by which to avoid the "real" world, as some literal-minded pragmatists have suggested, Kabbalah has very much to say to the world today, just as, conversely, many members of the scientific community can no longer be accused by metaphysicians of worshiping solely at the altar of "What Is." And in as much as the laws governing the metaphysical realms cannot and must not oppose those of the physical world — they are one and the same — it is becoming increasingly apparent that Kabbalah and Science might aptly be likened to two parallel streams that sprang from a common source and whose waters will once again mingle when they meet the sea.

Thus, the Circle will be complete.

-R. L. Fisher
July 28, 1986

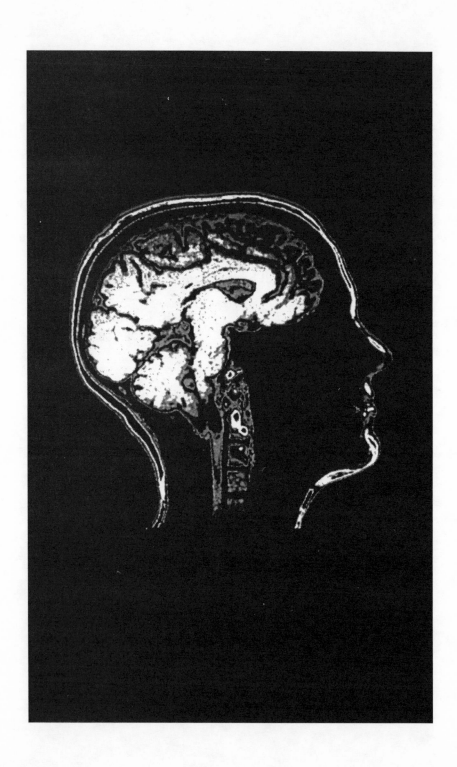

INTRODUCTION

THE GREATEST, MOST ADVANCED, COMPUTER ever conceived is not locked within the confines of a massive government vault. Nor is it the jealously guarded secret treasure of some chrome-eyed corporate giant. No, the greatest, most advanced and powerful computer that was ever invented is a strange looking thing that weights no more than a few pounds. With the outer casing removed, one might easily mistake it for a creature that just emerged from the depths of some fictional Black Lagoon. You have probably gathered that we are referring to that convoluted mass of nerves and tissue: The Human Brain.

Why, one might well ask, if I'm so smart, can't I tap into these vast reserves of potential energy and turn them to my advantage?

The answer is, you can. Before you venture into any unknown situation, though, common sense should dictate the wisdom of possessing as much knowledge as possible of the pitfalls and obstacles that might hamper your way.

Through the teachings of the masters we learned that the rational mind represents only a minute fraction of mankind's true potential. The infinitely more powerful, more dynamic circuitry in the human computer remains in suspended animation until such time as it is revitalized through the limited creative process known to Kabbalah as the Line. Consciously or unconsciously we are all searching for the software by which to access those vast reserves. Kabbalah is such a program.

As miraculous as it may seem, the computer operates on a binary system, which means that each of its circuits has but one operation to perform: on or off. Each of the tiny circuits within the computer is conducting electricity or not conducting it, depending on the given commands. On or off, positive or negative, restricting or not restricting, fulfilled or unfulfilled, such was the world view expressed by sixteenth century kabbalist, Isaac Luria, the creator of Lurianic Kabbalah. The computer, as remarkable an invention' as it is, obviously does not hold a candle to its inventor, the human brain.

The human computer is so far in advance of even the most powerful binary computing machine that comparison is hardly possible. The challenge we face is that of how to access those vast megabytes of potential energy and make them work for us. We have all of the necessary hardware, bits and bytes, all of the "read only" and "random access" systems necessary for our own unique fulfillment, but the conscious mind, a tiny fraction of our true potential, has taken over the controls. The effect is like having access to a thousand NASA computers, but the only disk you have to run them is the home version of Pac Man. Even the most advanced computer in the world is useless without an equally powerful program.

Learning Kabbalah is like slipping a powerful software system into the disk drive of our human computer. One does not become conversant with a program overnight. Depending on the complexity of the software, the documentation, support systems, and so forth, it can take weeks to become familiar with the basics of the system, and years until the various features have been mastered. Eventually, while we may not have the slightest idea of how the computer functions internally, the various functions become second nature so much so that when a new problem presents itself, we can sometimes even second guess the programmer.

Such is the nature of Kabbalah.

Little by little, through the program that is Kabbalah, we begin to grasp the four phases and their primary, secondary, and tertiary divisions. By understanding the computerized system, we establish the program which allows us to avoid many of the pitfalls made by those whose lives are ruled by trial and error. Instead of having to find a new solution for each and every obstacle set in our path, the kabbalistic frame of reference allows us to return to the root cause of each matter and thus avoid the constant interruptions presented by life in the material world.

And so it is that while the miracle of the human brain may remain forever beyond the scope of our reasoning abilities, we can, through the careful application of kabbalistic principles, acquire a sense of our own inner workings. For we are models of the universe, as it was, is, and will be, and by understanding the microcosm that is us we connect with the macrocosm that is the Or En Sof, the infinite power of the universe.

1

THE THOUGHT OF CREATION

IN THE BEGINNING, BEFORE THE UNIVERSE became the multi-universe that we live in today, there existed an Infinite "circular" condition of mutual fulfillment between the Light (Emanator/Creator) and the Vessel (Emanated/Created). The Light found completion by giving endlessly of its beneficence and the vessels (though as yet in an undifferentiated state) experienced total satisfaction at receiving endlessly of the Light's supreme positiveness.

This Infinite "circular" condition was disturbed by a stirring within the emanated beings known to Kabbalah as Bread of Shame. No longer could the emanated vessels partake endlessly of unearned benevolence and so, to absolve Bread of Shame, they asked and were granted a share in the give and take of creation. The Light, whose only desire was to share, saw fit to restrict or withdraw its Infinite illumination so that another desire, the Desire to Receive could manifest.

From this restriction, or contraction of the Light, known to kabbalists as the Tsimtsum (zim-zum) and to modern science as the Big Bang, was born the multi-universe with all its variety and individuation, and never again would the vessel find true fulfillment in taking that which was not earned. Hence it is said that the Light gave birth to darkness, the Circle to the Line.

HOW THE CIRCLE BECAME A LINE

For the kabbalist the sphere and the circle are symbols rich in nuance and meaning. The sphere is an example of perfect symmetry, for no matter from which angle it is viewed the image remains the same. The circle, a one dimensional representation of remains the same. The circle, a one dimensional representation of the sphere, symbolizes Infinity. Having no beginning and no end, it stands too for the unity, completeness and perfection that was the domain of En Sof before the withdrawal and restriction (Tsimtsum), and which will again be the universal condition when this current age of correction has completed its cycle.

The Ari, Rabbi Isaac Luria, described in fine detail the ways in which the ten circular vessels (Sefirot) were revealed after the Tsimtsum and how the Sefirot receive Light from the Line. It is important not to limit ourselves to a literal interpretation of the concepts revealed to us by the Ari, but rather to try to draw from them their metaphysical implications. Consider, then, the Circle and the Line as a convenient method by which to metaphorically illustrate that which might otherwise be a difficult or even impenetrable subject.

Unlike the Circle, the Line has a beginning, a middle, and end. So while the Circle represents Infinity, the Line serves to conceptually illuminate that which is finite. And whereas the universal condition that existed before the Tsimtsum is described as being in circular form, meaning there was complete unity between the Creator and that which He had created, the condition after the restriction took on a Finite, linear dimension, and hence is represented by the Line. The Line, in other words, permits us to have a conceptual idea of limitation which is not possible with the Circle.

In the beginning there was no distinction between the Creator and the Created, the Light and the Vessel, the Circle and the Line. All different concepts, all different entities, all different energy-intelligences were unified. That is not to say there were no differences between them. And herein lies a fine distinction which we in this fragmented world find difficult to comprehend: There were variables, but they were not yet manifested. The myriad elements, entities, and energies were present in the En Sof before the restriction but they did not yet express themselves as separate manifestations.

2

MAKING METAPHYSICAL CONNECTIONS

HEBREW THEOLOGY WAS BUILT UPON THREE distinct and equally firm foundations. The first was the law which was known to all citizens of Israel. The second was the oral tradition, Mishna, *the soul of the law*, which was known only by Rabbis and teachers. The third, Kabbalah, *the soul of the soul of the law*, was revealed to only a chosen few.

The roots of Kabbalah go deep into the soil of man's primordial past. Certain individuals, it seems, have always sought to reach beyond the grasp of intellect to establish a link with a higher reality; there have always been seekers of an apprehension of the Infinite for whom face value was not enough. Even the most ancient cave paintings, pictographs and petroglyphs attest to man's belief in mystical linkages, myths, and magical transformations. There have always been, and there will always be, those who seek to find the word within the word, the thought within the thought, the meaning within the meaning.

Judging by the preponderance of evidence, it would seem that an excellent case could be made for mystical transcendence being a basic human need. Yet mention an occult or mystical subject to the man on the street today and you are libel to be met with derisive comments, mocking laughter, with perhaps a bar or two of the theme from The *Twilight Zone* tossed in for good measure. "It's not rational," they might be apt to say. "It's not real." If they can't taste it, touch it, see it with their own two eyes, for them it does not exist. Yet what is gravity but an unseen force for which we have no rational explanation? And what of magnetism? We can't see it; we can't explain it; but does that mean it's not there?

When a fool sees a well-dressed person, he looks no further. But the thinking man knows that the worth of the clothes has nothing to do with the body that is robed in them. While the kabbalist knows that the worth of the body is in the soul that abides in it. Just as the sheen and ripples on the surface of the water hide that which lies beneath the surface, so too does empirical existence obscure divine reality.

THE REAL WORLD

"Get real," is an expression one is apt to hear today. It means that the speaker has a better grasp of reality than the person to whom he or she is speaking. It might be followed by other hard line materialist phrases such as: "The truth of the matter..." or, "The bottom line is..." and ended with punch lines such as, "It's every man for himself," "They're playing hardball out there," and the old chestnut, "Only the strong survive."

The real world, it seems, is a place of rocks and hard places. Gone is the mystery, the paradox, the irony. Reality is the "thing" today. Nearly everyone these days will hasten to tell us all we want to know about reality and a lot more that we might rather not know. Politicians, businessmen, prostitutes, grocery clerks, and banana republic dictators all swear up and down that they live in the real world. Yet when asked for a definition of reality each gives a different answer.

For the rich man it is a place of comfort, refinement, and opulence. For the working man it is a place where one struggles to make a living. For the man who is starving it is a hell from which the only escape is death. The real world is a place where you shut your mouth, do your job, and take the money. A place of hard knocks and grindstones to which we must keep our noses. A place where righteous people pull themselves up by the bootstraps and "make something of themselves."

But what is it really?

The confusion arises because there are two real worlds.

One is the "real" world of illusion, examples of which are given above. All things of this earthly realm are a part of the illusionary reality. It is a reality that changes with the tides, becoming larger and smaller, harder and softer, faster and slower, depending on how it is perceived. It is a world of symptoms and appearances, starvation and despair, elegance, opulence, and illusionary grandeur. It is many things to many people. In the end it might be said that it is anything you want to make it, and, hence, not real at all. The other is the reality of the *Or En Sof,* the Light of Creation. This reality is changeless, complete, eternal and Infinite. Beyond the realm of struggle and restriction, lies and deceit, illusion, desire and petty machinations — it is a place of peace and perfection, a place of stillness and ultimate, primal truth.

The two realities are separated by a hair's breadth, apart from each other yet together all the same. One, this earthly realm, is called the Lower World, the other is called the Upper. One is coarse, the other is fine, one is dense, the other lighter than space, one, the Upper World, is hidden, the Lower World is revealed. It is said that there are two sides to every story. Kabbalah mediates between them. The kabbalist's task is to resolve them both.

WHAT YOU SEE IS WHAT YOU FORGET

Every North American is familiar with the expression, "I'm from Missouri." It might aptly be translated as, "Show me," or "I'll believe it only if I see it with my own two eyes." It implies that the person who is speaking is a "realist" over whose eyes the wool cannot easily be pulled. Expressions such a these attest to the pride we place in our ability to "see the world as it really is."

In truth, Missouri would certainly be a sorry place if all the people there were to limit their comprehension of existence based solely on what they could see. Words such a *faith, hope, love, and intuition* would have to be removed from the dictionary. All religions would have to be abolished, for how many of us can attest to having truly seen God? Theories involving quarks, quasars, black holes, and subatomic particles would have to be dropped from the scientific lexicon — not to mention electromagnetism, germs, and atoms. And as if all this were not bad enough, they would even have to repeal the Law of Gravity.

The point is, our five senses are notoriously bad judges of the world around us. We all have, no doubt, been in a situation in which a sound is heard and every person in the room believes that sound came from a different place. The sense of taste and the closely related sense of smell can be easily fooled by chemical scents and additives. Nor is the sense of touch any better at gauging actuality, as any number of college pranks involving a blindfold, an ice cube, and the suggestion of fire, can attest. Taste, touch, smell, sight, hearing — all of our senses play tricks on us. Why then do we place so much faith in them? Where do we turn to find the truth?

The physical world is an illusion; the real world is one step beyond. To comprehend the nature of the physical world it is imperative that we begin making perceptual connections with the metaphysical realm. By the same token, to comprehend the nature of the external world, it is necessary to connect with the internal. Just because something is seen with the eyes does not mean that it exists any more than not seeing something is proof that it does not exist. Through Kabbalah we peel away the layers of illusion 50 that we may connect to the Light within.

3

OR EN SOF

OR EN SOF, THE LIGHT OF CREATION, PLAYS AT the edge of our consciousness like a dream that cannot quite be remembered. Moments before waking there is a crucial instant when only a loose thread connects the dreamer with his dream. The harder the dreamer pulls on that delicate strand the more quickly does the fabric of the dream unravel and disappear. Try as he might to reattach the thread, his dream fades and the dreamer must resolve himself to a waking "reality" immensely inferior to that of his dream.

We all have experienced some form of what might be called supernatural communication, moments of intense rapture or lucidity that far exceed the run-of-the-mill perceptions with which we normally attend to in our daily routines. For some those brief interludes of expanded consciousness become the fuel of obsessions. Returning to those ecstatic moments becomes the sole focus of their lives. They may search in drugs and vicarious thrills, in war and sexual conquests, in speed, thievery, and other modes of dangerous behavior, but though it is true that brief flashes of cosmic awareness may accompany such activities, those fleeting moments of insight soon evaporate into nothing more than pale recollections. Instead of achieving any lasting result, people who engage in such activities must constantly raise the stakes of their adventures in order to realize a lesser degree of stimulation than that which was attained before.

Metaphysical connections are by their very nature illusory — so much so that most of us acquiesce to a life without them. Though those brief encounters with the next dimensions provide evidence of a world so superior to this phase of existence that comparison is hardly possible, having no words to describe our experiences, and no validation from traditional sources of the existence of the higher realms, we banish the memories of our extraterrestrial sojourns to hidden catacombs deep in our unconscious minds.

Many people attend houses of worship regularly without ever having anything approaching a religious experience. While they may derive some small comfort from a feeling that "something is out there,1 something magnificent and all-encompassing, their belief in this otherworldly entity, or extraterrestrial intelligence, provides consolation, but not contentment, for it is only something to believe in and not something to connect with. Being unaware of its existence these people have no reason to create a link with energy-intelligence of the cosmos. The majority of people go through life unaware that the *Or En Sof* could be theirs for the asking, never comprehending the psychological and spiritual discomforts it could quell, the inner needs it would more than gladly fulfill. For them the metaphysical world, if they even acknowledge its existence, seems totally divorced of useful function. Hence, they live their lives, little knowing that it is their the lack of attachment with the higher realms of consciousness that is the sole determining factor for the quiet desperation in which they must continually exist.

Like a dream that cannot quite be remembered, the *Or En Sof* dances at the fringes of our conscious minds. Kabbalah is a way to connect with that dream which is a reality. Like a single taste of the most exquisite delicacy, the *Or En Sof* tickles the palate of our collective and individual consciousness, and whether we know it or not, our unconscious minds are constantly striving to find the source of that taste and possibly even learn the recipe. Kabbalah is such a recipe. Through Kabbalah we discover the means by which to bring the *Or En Sof* to our earthly table, so that we may partake of a constant diet of unearthly delights.

4

THE SEED

ANY STUDENT OF KABBALAH WILL BENEFIT from a metaphorical examination of the seed. Like Jack's magic beans, the seed can serve as a conceptual link with the upper worlds; and like the Giant's key, the seed can reveal the jewels of wisdom which can only be discovered by knowledge of the inner truth. And certainly, at least on this physical plane of existence, there can be no better example than the seed for describing the *En Sof* before the Thought of Creation.

Within the seed, as with the *En Sof* before the restriction, there exists the potential for roots, leaves, branches, and blossoms. We can look at the seed of an apple and say, here are the roots, here is the bark, here are the branches, the leaves, and the apples. Here is both the Desire to Receive as well as the Desire to Impart, the Light and the Vessel, the Circle and the Line. And just as the unplanted seed replicates in some way the conditions inherent in the *En Sof* before the restriction, the seed, when planted, stands as an example of the conditions as they existed after the withdrawal and resulting contraction.

Only after various conditions are met (moisture, soil, sunlight) can the chain of events begin which will allow the undifferentiated elements within the seed to express themselves as separate entities. Let us at this stage examine the prevailing conditions within the *En Sof* before the Tsimtsum in order that we may better understand the chain of events which allowed the seed of creation, so to speak, to blossom.

BEFORE THE BIG BANG

All ten of the divine Sefirot or Luminous Emanations (bottled-up energy-intelligences) were present within the Endless World from which sprang all future worlds. A perfect balance existed between the endless imparting of the Creator and the endless receiving of his creations — the souls of man. This condition of unity might have gone on forever had it not been for an aspiration towards equality which was inherent in the Will to Receive. It was this desire to be a part of the give and take of Creation which resulted in the Tsimtsum.

The souls of man felt ashamed at the one-sidedness of their relationship with the Creator. This condition, which results from receiving that which is not earned, is defined in kabbalistic terms as Bread of Shame. And as it was the Creator's wish, and sole purpose, to bestow abundance on his creations, and as his creations could partake of His abundance only to the degree to which their sense of shame would allow them, the Creator caused the

perfect Will to Receive to undergo a contraction (Tsimtsum) thereby causing a diversity of phase (separation) between the Emanator and the emanated, "severing or discriminating the latter from the Former and causing the emanated one to acquire its own particular name."

Thus, did the Creator withdraw so that the Infinite could give birth to the finite, the Circle to the Line, the Seed of Creation to the Tree of Life. That moment of divine conception, known to kabbalists as the Thought of Creation, and to scientists as the Big Bang, was the root of creation, the source from which the Universe expanded, complete with all of its phases and diversity, physical and metaphysical, as it was, is, and forever will be. As the seed contains the tree, the Thought of Creation contained the Tree of Life. The effect is always contained within the cause. The end result is inherent at the inception. To grasp this is to grasp a kabbalistic absolute; to master it is to find true wisdom.

BEFORE AND AFTER

Rabbi Isaac Luria taught us that fulfillment is the cause of desire, not the other way around. Nothing ever comes into existence the roots of which have not taken hold in the ten circular sefirot. Desire was born from the Upper Light and to the *Or En Sof* it yearns to return. Our inner encircling vessels will find no rest unless and until all of the Infinite (Circular) Illumination which was once revealed in them shines with the same luminous intensity as it did long ago in the place without end.

Having pondered this wisdom, the Ari advanced a concept, elegant in its simplicity, that all phases of existence can be encompassed by a conceptual construct involving only two phases

or conditions. The first phase consists of Desire that is fulfilled —
as epitomized by the universal condition before Tsimtsum. The
second phase includes Desire that is unfulfilled — as exemplified
by all that happened after Tsimtsum. The condition of fulfillment
he called The Endless World. The latter condition of unfulfillment he named The World of Restriction.

By thus limiting the scope of existence the Ari had arrived,
at a formula that had validity for every conceivable subject and situation. All of humanity's trials and tribulations, all life and
growth, every thought, word, deed, and physical manifestation
can be explained and understood according to which phase of
Desire (fulfilled or unfulfilled) that is presently being revealed.
Desire is constantly seeking fulfillment just as Light is endlessly
available for revealment.

From this perspective there seems to be only one question
that is truly worth asking: Am I revealing the Light or am I con-
cealing It?

THE CLOSER THE BETTER

The seed is stronger than the tree. The root is stronger
than the branch. The Circle is stronger than the Line. The Light
is stronger than the Vessel. The thought is stronger than the word.
The cause is stronger than the effect. The baby is stronger than
the man.

What is meant by all this?

That which is closer to the source is said to be stronger,
higher, loftier. The Light contained the Vessel as the cause con-

tains the effect. The seed knows everything about the tree, the roots and branches have a more limited perspective. A baby is born with every brain cell that he or she will ever possess. Spiritually the baby has fewer complications than the man, fewer veils, less klippot. It is said that prophecy exists by imbeciles and children, and scientists tell us that the physical body begins to die the moment we are born.

So what is stronger?

That which is closest to the source.

5

THE ILLUSION OF DARKNESS

WHEN THE CREATOR WITHDREW FROM THE
endless in order that free will could have expression and we, the
emanated, could be absolved of the Bread of Shame, He left a vacuum and the illusion of darkness. For all earthly intents and purposes, it seemed that the ten Luminous Emanations had disap-
peared. Yet we know that it is a keystone of kabbalistic thought
and theory that every word and every action, every manifestation,
internal and external, physical and metaphysical, is imbued with
the Light of Creation. How, then, can there be darkness?

In reality, the Light, which had formerly illuminated all
phases of the Endless with equal magnitude, had been transformed and made manifest in a finite or linear form. Earlier we
described the Light of Creation before the restriction as existing in
circular form, while after the Tsimtsum the vessels (Sefirot) containing the Light of Creation are said to have taken on the shape

of a Line. The Circular Sefirot transformed, becoming the Sefirot of Straightness.

The Vessels and the Light contained within them became obscured from our view as a result of negativity which might accurately be described as a by-product of the Desire to Receive. This negative energy, known as Klippot (Husks or Shells), encircled the Light and the Vessels at the moment of the Thought of Restriction, producing an effect similar to that of a curtain placed over a lamp. The light is there in all its glory, but the viewer doesn't see it and so is unaware that it even exists. Thus, do the veils or metaphysical barriers cloud our perceptions and limit our spiritual potential.

The ten Circular Sefirot, then, did not disappear. There is no disappearance in the realm of the metaphysical. Radical, essential changes only occur within material objects and in the perceptions of man. The shape of the vessels changed, but not the nature of the "bottled-up energy" within.

The same may be said of the seed that grew into a tree. The same may be said of the Circle that turned into a Line. The same may be said of the Light that transformed into Darkness. They are all there — we just don't see them.

PERSPECTIVES

"One man's floor is another man's ceiling."
"One man's trash is another man's treasure."
"One man's art is another man's eyesore."

These old adages speak clearly of perspectives. Indeed, beauty, ugliness, and everything in between, are in the eye of the beholder. Our reality is shaped to a large degree by our point of view. Take as an example a situation in which three people, a small child, a man of average height, and a man of exceptional height, gaze upon the same statue at a museum. If later asked to describe the statute the small child might comment on the chin or beard, (assuming the statue was of a man), while the man  of average height might comment on the face or eyes, and the exceptionally tall man might comment on the part of the hair.

There that statue sits, a solid, formed, material object of hardest steel or stone, and yet it means something completely different to everyone who sees it.

Is the same not true of all material objects? Taking this argument one step further might not the same be said of the entire material world? Is reality just a matter of perspective? You might arrive at that conclusion. It all depends on your point of view.

THE TWO FACES OF DESIRE

Kabbalah classifies the Sefirot into two categories: The Encircling Sefirot and the Sefirot of Straightness. Before Tsimtsum, the circular vessels were eternally satiated with the Light of Creation. The Restriction created a condition in which the Infinite Light contained within the Encircling Sefirot would remain concealed until acted upon by the Sefirot of Straightness, an aspect of the Line. The Circular Sefirot originated within the *En Sof* and at the time of the Tsimtsum, whereas the Sefirot of Straightness were an outgrowth of the subsequent limited creative process, the Line. Therefore the Encircling Sefirot are considered superior, purer by virtue of their closer proximity to the Endless.

The Encircling Vessels cannot and must not receive Illumination in the Infinite sense, otherwise all Desire (negativity), and consequently all opportunity for correction, would be inundated by the omnipotent Light of the En Sol. In that event the original purpose of Creation would be defeated, as the Light would engulf the vessel and the universe would revert to its original condition with the undifferentiated energy-intelligences receiving endlessly of the Light's beneficence, but again experiencing a sense of dissatisfaction at having no way of absolving Bread of Shame.

Desire has two faces. One, the Desire to Receive for the Sake of Sharing, is an attribute of the Circle. The second, the Desire to Receive for Oneself Alone, is a characteristic of the Line. Desire is humanity's most important asset in the struggle for physical survival, but it is also the largest obstacle on the path toward personal and planetary redemption. It is our most negative trait, but also our greatest opportunity for correction. By Restricting the negative side of Desire we create a circular concept (an affinity or similarity of form between the Light and the Vessel) and thereby convert the negative aspect of Desire into the positive aspect.

The Sefirot of Circles provide the impetus for all activity in the World of Restriction. They initiate all of our unconscious yearnings to return to our original Infinite condition. Were it not for those vague, primal memories of our past fulfillment being indelibly etched in our circular vessels we would be totally devoid of all longing and desire — which would greatly hasten the extinction of the human race.

We of Malkhut can find no peace until the Light contained within the Encircling Sefirot has been restored to its former brilliance. That possibility, however, in this phase of existence, is remote in the extreme. The finite nature of the Sefirot of Straightness precludes the possibility of them filling our Encircling Vessels to their fullest capacity, for as we know, that which is finite can never equal that which is Infinite.

Still, true and lasting fulfillment can be attained in this the World of Restriction — but not Infinite perfection. According to the ancient texts the complete Illumination of WI of the Encircling Vessels will occur only when the corrective process has come full circle.

6

THE SEFIROT OF STRAIGHTNESS

THE VESSELS OF THE TEN SEFIROT OF
straightness are called Pipes because they limit and control with
great precision the Light drawn through them. Just as the capacity
of a pipe is gauged by its diameter and the volume of water that
can flow through it, so too do kabbalists measure the capacity of
the Sefirot of Straightness. The Light, the *Or En Sof*, flows
through the Vessels of Straightness in exact proportion to the
Vessel's degree of longing, just as water flows through a pipe
according to that vessel's capacity.

The Ari, in his description of "The Line as a Narrow Pipe"
makes use of two phrases which the student of Kabbalah may find
confusing. He refers to "the waters of the Upper Light" ad later
makes reference to "the more important Light" being "clothed in
the purer vessel." As for the former, simply stated, when Light
descends from its level in !he manner that water descends via grav-

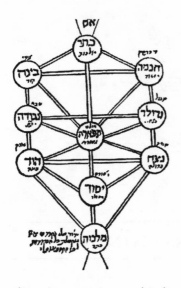

ity, it takes on the image of waters of Light. The "more important" Light, in the latter phrase, mentioned as being "clothed in the purer vessel" refers to the Light which is "more important" and the Vessel "purer" by virtue of being closer (having a greater affinity) with the Endless.

In more personal terms, a person who has a great degree of Desire to Receive for the Sake of Sharing will receive of the Light in direct proportion to his longing, whereas the person who has little or no Desire to Impart will receive little or no Light. The latter would not be entirely wrong in stating that there is no Creator or grand design, because for him they do not exist.

In the same manner that children sometimes attempt to hide from their playmates by covering their eyes with their hands, so too does the negative person hide from the Light of Creation. And just as a child who finally wearies of the darkness may peek through the cracks between his fingers, so 100 can a negative person, in a manner of speaking, open the fingers of his or her being and see the Light — the amount or magnitude of which will be directly proportionate to the size of the opening.

Stress, neuroses, burn-out, these terms from the modern vernacular describe conditions in which the flow of energy is uneven. If the inward flow is too great or too little the pipe is apt to burst or become so corroded as to allow no energy to pass through. An even flow of energy is essential to a person's physical, emotional, and spiritual well being.

You will recall that before the Tsimtsum, Bread of Shame caused the Vessel to deny the endless flow of Divine Energy ad this denial brought about the Restriction which granted a degree of free will to the Vessels. Henceforth, it became the universal condition that the Light would flow according to the instructions given to it by the Vessel. From that moment on it became our responsibility to control the input valves of our own creation.

LIGHT

The Light can be both a shield and a weapon. Not that the Light of Creation can be wielded like a sword or shot like a gun, for no mortal being can presume to actually control the Light of Creation. The Light, however, whose desire is to share, achieves full expression only in the presence of a desire to receive, and should that receiving desire be motivated by the right intentions the true purpose of both Light and Vessel can be achieved.

The Light, the *Or En Sof*, accepts the direction of the Vessel in a manner similar to the way sunlight, or artificial light, can be directed through a fine strand, or vessel, of fiber optical material. And just as a solar panel either attracts, repels, or magnifies sunlight according to the purpose for which it has been adjusted, so too can we, through the "darkness or lightness" of our purpose and intentions, attract, repel, and otherwise give expression to the *Or En Sof*.

If a child cannot sleep because he or she is afraid of darkness, the symptomatic solution, of course, is to turn on the lights. That will alleviate the problem temporarily, but to relieve the symptoms permanently it becomes necessary to reveal the source of the problem, the metaphysical cause. Only by bringing the child's fears into the open, can the parent help the child to understand that it is not really the darkness that the child is afraid of, but that which he or she imagines to be lurking in the darkness. Perhaps it is fear of ghosts, goblins, bogey men, or the recollections of some horrific television villain, that is causing the child's insomnia. A patient explanation that his or her fears are unfounded, sheds light on the metaphysical root cause of the child's problem, and, in so doing, helps the child effect a permanent cure.

Solar energy harbors great hope for mankind, but there is absolutely no hope of man ever making the slightest change in the sun itself. The same may be said for the *Or En Sof* . Light will accept direction, but the eternal circle of creation cannot be altered in any way by man, it cannot be brightened or dimmed, chemically transformed, genetically grafted, or split like an atom. The reality of its divine existence is complete, eternal, Infinite — change occurs only in the fleeting perceptions of man.

Darkness, in the material world, cannot exist in the presence of light. Nor can metaphysical darkness exist in the presence of the Energy-Intelligence known as the Light of Creation. Those who attract Light for the sake of sharing attract Illumination of sufficient amplitude to enlighten even the darkest corners of their beings. This method by which Light is attracted for the purpose of imparting, transforms negative into positive, evil into good, darkness into Light.

7

By Any Other Name

STUDENTS OF KABBALAH ARE OFTEN confused and exasperated by the seeming plethora of terms used to describe what at first appears to be the same concept. For instance, the expressions: Crown, Wisdom, Intelligence, Beauty, and Kingdom describe the condition in the Encircling Sefirot after the Light had withdrawn (Tsimtsum) and only the impressions (residues or vibrations) remained. The terms Living, Soul, Spirit, and Individual, on the other hand, are employed to describe the same Vessels after they have been restored with Light. Add to this confusing array, "The Five Worlds" or "Extensions of Emanation:" Primordial, Emanation, Creation, Formation, and Action — as well as the "four phases," Light, Water, Firmament, and One Hundred Blessings, also called "Lights of the Soul" and "Levels of Consciousness," which refer to the four grades of the Desire to Receive.

Thousands more examples could be given, but it is not our purpose to confuse the reader further, but merely to give a brief overview of Kabbalah's rich linguistic heritage and some of the reasons for its development. The highly complex language of Kabbalah evolved slowly over a millennium in response to ever-widening, deepening knowledge of the nature of man's intimate relationship with the cosmos. It continues to develop, expand, and ripen to this day.

The kabbalist's task is by no means an easy one: Using illusionary symbols — both in the sense that all languages are symbolic and therefore illusionary, and also in kabbalistic sense that all things of this world are illusion, hence language, too, must be unreal — he attempts to provide a reasonable explanation for that which is beyond reason, to give expression to that which cannot be expressed, to illuminate concepts that are beyond the range of the senses. And, as if that were not enough, he must do all this with words that already have other fixed connotations and denotations that are often the antithesis of the concepts he is trying to express.

Is it any wonder that not everyone can understand what the kabbalist has to say? Pragmatists criticize the language of Kabbalah as being irrational and illogical, and from their narrow perspective they are, of course, quite correct. In fact, the kabbalist would be the first to admit it, for one of the main purposes of Kabbalah is to transcend what is commonly called "logic" and "rationality" so that the real world can be perceived.

Needless to say, then, the study of Kabbalah is not for those who are extremely literal-minded. Rooted as they are in the illusion we call Malkhut, the so-called rationalist is incapable of

צט) בההוא ז זמנא, יתער מלכא משיחא, מ לנפקא
מההוא אתר דאתקרי ק"ן צפו"ר, ויתער בארעא
דגליל, וההוא יומא דיפוק לתמן, יתרגז כל עלמא
וכל בני עלמא מתחבאין גו מערתי וטנרי,דלאיחשבון
לאשתזבא. ועל ההוא זמנא כתיב, ה) ובאו במערות

A Passage from the Zohar in Aramaic

making the conceptual leap to the Divine word of Infinity from the limited language of Man. Logic cannot arrive at a conclusion that is beyond the realm of logic. Nor can the kabbalist's language be heard by those who do not know how to listen. Words, thoughts, and ideas amount to nothing unless their meanings are understood.

The language of Kabbalah is of necessity a finite and therefore limited expression, but the concepts of Kabbalah, the indelible truths, can be comprehended by those who read the Language of the Branches with their hearts and not just with their eyes, and who listen with their minds and not just their ears.

It is hoped that the reader now fully understands the need for various nomenclatures to clarify numerous layers of symbolic meaning.

8

THE CAUSE CONTAINS THE EFFECT

IN THE FIRST CHAPTER OF THE SECOND
volume of "Ten Luminous Emanations", the Ari states that,
"Everything which is Desire on an Upper Level is Necessity on a
Lower Level emanated by its Upper Cause." He was speaking of
cause and effect. The words "Upper" and "Lower" do not refer in
this instance to actual physical relationships, but rather to that
which is closer to (Upper) or farther (Lower) from the source. And
so it is when the kabbalist says that "not even a blade of grass
exists in this world without having its roots in the phase above" he
is referring to that which happens at one stage being the result of
that which happened one stage before.

Just as the leaf of a maple tree cannot suddenly decide one
day to become the leaf of an aspen, nor an apple tree to become
an orange tree, a man too must exist within the context of certain
predestined genetic and cultural parameters. The tree is the effect

contained within the cause which is the seed, just as a man is the effect contained within the cause that was the "seed" of his parents, just as this world, Malkhut, is the effect contained within its Upper cause, Formation.

That the effect is contained within the cause is, along with the idea of Endlessness, one of the most difficult metaphysical principles for the rational thinker to comprehend. The answer, as was stated in a previous chapter, is that nothing of a metaphysical nature can be experienced by the five senses. However, it is hoped that the examples given will allow the student to make the proper metaphysical connections. To the examples given, namely the leaf and the seed, and the parent and the child, add one more example, that of the "life" of a baseball which is thrown at a plate glass window.

Momentum, in a way of speaking, is a messenger of the energy-intelligence which, in this case, started the baseball in motion. Energy, as science has proven, has mass. Thoughts are energy, therefore they have mass, therefore they are palpable things. The ball becomes a living thing whose purpose is predestined by the person who threw it. The desire of the thrower becomes necessity on the lower (later) level emanated by its upper (earlier) cause, and somehow this moving energy-intelligence telegraphs its trajectory to the object at which it is aimed, and the object, in our example a plate glass window, responds by beginning to break up even before the ball reaches it. This phenomenon has been scientifically validated using microscopic photography, but has yet to be explained.

Could it be that the energy-intelligence which caused the ball to be thrown precedes the ball to its destination?

If so, it follows that cause and effect, instead of being considered as two separate entities, must now be considered as two parts of a single entity, one contained within the other. Hence we say that the cause contains the effect, which translates for modern ears the ancient, and far more poetic, adage: *He and His Name are One*. He being the Creator or the cause, and *His Name*, being the Vessel or effect, are inseparable. Like space-time, and mass-energy, cause and effect are one and the same.

FULFILLMENT

Our denial of the Creator's endless imparting, which resulted in the Tsimtsum, caused the Sefirot of Circles to be left with but a mere impression of their former Illumination. Before the Tsimtsum the existence of an independent Desire to Receive was an impossibility, for any desire that might have manifested would have been instantly satisfied. The Light still shines brightly within us, but because of Tsimtsum we have lost touch with It. Eclipsed by the negative trappings of physical existence, the Light, the source of that divine memory, for all worldly intents and purposes, remains latent and only potentially active.

Every one of us, with the possible exception of those who are blessed, or some might say cursed, with a photographic memory, has developed patterns of behavior around important psychological events that we have forgotten. Hidden deep in the subconsciousness these memories affect every aspect of our lives. Such is the case with the memory possessed by all mankind of our unity with the *Or En Sof*. The effect remains but not the cause.

Like echoes in a canyon, like muffled whispers in some

foreign tongue, like phrases that can't quite be remembered, those nebulous impressions of our former unity with the *Or En Sof* haunt and sometimes irritate us. Unconsciously, unknowingly, the impressions link us with the supreme fulfillment that was ours before the Tsimtsum and keep us on our restless search for contentment.

Fulfillment is illusive. One can search a lifetime and never attain it. As ephemeral as a dream, it hovers near the outskirts of consciousness, barely out of grasp. As rare and priceless as an artistic masterpiece, true satisfaction is something that for most of us can only be appreciated from a distance. Like the Mona Lisa it is not for sale, but even if it were it would be way beyond our current spiritual means.

Lasting fulfillment escapes most of us for the simple reason that we each have but one true calling, one quest, venture, or undertaking that will permanently illuminate our seemingly vacant encircling vessels. This unique ordination was revealed to all of us in the *En Sof* with the Thought of Creation. The challenge faced by each of us is to rediscover the endeavor or singular activity that will once more establish our affinity with the Light.

The revealment of the latent *Or En Sof* within us can be accomplished in one of two ways. One is the trial and error approach in which the seeker tries on new lifestyles, philosophies, diets and spiritual doctrines as readily as a fashion model changes hats. Though not impossible, the odds against finding enduring fulfillment in this manner are monumental. A far less haphazard approach requires an understanding of the process of mental, emotional, and spiritual evolution as taught by Kabbalah.

All that lives and breathes takes part in an identical evolutionary process. Every manifestation, physical and metaphysical, advances through the same four stages in the universal quest toward completion. When correctly perceived and applied, the teachings of Kabbalah let us see at a glance the stage through which any entity or manifestation is passing, up to and including ourselves.

This world is an illusion. The real world is hidden from view by veils of negativity, symptoms, and appearances. Through Kabbalah we gain new insights that allow us to trace the Line that is our lives back to our primordial beginnings in the *En Sof* where we were once unified with the Circle of Creation. Thus, do we reveal the Light of the Endless anew.

SYMPATHETIC VIBRATIONS

Every vessel has a certain note that causes it to reverberate louder than at any other frequency. Gently encircle the rim of a wine glass with a moistened finger to find that vessel's resonant harmonic. The singer's trick of breaking wine glasses is accomplished by singing that particular pitch at a volume sufficient to cause the glass to explode from the force of its own vibrations. By singing an ascending or descending scale into any container the one resonant harmonic can be readily identified that will cause the vessel to reverberate most loudly in sympathy with the note being sung.

The same can be said for the vessel that is our soul. One note, one activity, one calling, more than any other, can cause our interior encircling vessels to come alive with sympathetic vibrations — the same resonant harmonic that once filled our encircling vessels when we were all but undifferentiated aspects of the universal music of the spheres. To find this one resonant harmonic is the key to contentment and satisfaction.

9

THE CIRCLE IS NOT ATTACHED TO THE ENDLESS

THE ABOVE PHRASE, ATTRIBUTED TO THE ARI, Rabbi Isaac Luria, cannot be taken at face value. As with all of the Ari's teachings, the meaning here cannot be grasped through literal interpretation. The reader is by now aware that Bread of Shame was the first cause of physical creation. The act of Tsimtsum dictated that the Circle and the Line would henceforth forever remain separated. From the moment that we, the emanated, asked for and received individuation from the Circle of the Endless, any and all revealment of the *Or En Sof* would, and could, only come about as a result of the Desire to Receive which is represented by the Line.

Otherwise, were it any other way, the Circle would embrace the Line, obliterating the essential dissimilarity of form that keeps the emanated separate from the Emanator, the Line from the Circle, the Vessel from the Light. And thus would the universe revert to its former state.

Attachment, from the kabbalistic frame of reference, pertains to similitude of form, or unity, whereas, diversity of phase, refers to detachment, or disunity. The words "not attached" in the above-mentioned phrase refer to this disunity between the Endless and the Sefira of the Crown of the Line which is the "Root" of the extension of the Light to the four emanations: Wisdom, Intelligence, Beauty, and this world, Kingdom. As a newborn child is still considered a part of its mother even though the umbilical cord may have been severed, so too are the Sefira of the Crown of Circles, still a part of, though apart from the Light of the Endless.

NEGATIVE EXPECTATIONS

Why do some men soar like eagles while others must burrow like moles. Why do some seem to drive straight to their destination while others meet with an endless variety of roadblocks and detours? Luck? Fate? Circumstances? Yes, perhaps each of these is in some way responsible. Yet members of the so-called Untouchable class have risen to high positions in the Indian government. Every day, it seems, we hear of someone, somewhere who has transcended the meanest of circumstances to achieve prominence and prosperity. Though it must be admitted that those fortunate individuals remain the exception rather than the rule.

Why is it that some seem destined to accept their lowly fate while others come much closer to reaching their full potential? Societal and familial obstacles? Lack of opportunity? Peer group pressure? Certainly these all play a part. At one time it was a known fact that the world was flat and anyone who had the temerity to suggest otherwise would be summarily burned at the stake. In more recent times there were those who predicted with absolute certainty that the Wright Brothers would never fly. "If God had meant man to fly he'd have given us wings," went their reasoning. Others warned Henry Ford that his plan to build the Model T would result in a disaster of the highest magnitude. No, they were not worried about pollution and the environment. The problem you see, was that the human body would disintegrate at speeds in excess of fifteen miles per hour. There have always been doomsayers and Doubting Thomases and thank heaven, there have always been those who refused to listen to them.

For decades runners strove in vain to conquer the Four-Minute-Mile. Again there were those who claimed that illusive mark to be beyond the scope of human capability. Then came Roger Bannister. Anyone who saw Mr. Bannister's historical record-breaking run will remember the look of agonized anguish etched into the runner's features as he crossed the finish line. Shortly after Roger Bannister broke the Four-Minute-Mile, another runner broke it, and another, and another. Today we watch runners being interviewed after having run a Sub-Four-Minute-mile, talking to the commentator as if they had been watching the race from the sidelines rather than having run in it. To what can we attribute the ease with which today's runners break a mark that was long thought impossible? Training? Nutrition? Equipment? Perhaps to some small degree — but a far more plausible reason is that the runners of today are not burdened, as Roger Bannister was, with the added weight of negative expectations.

Negative expectations depend entirely upon the individuals' attachment or detachment from the Circle. The Light contains an energy-intelligence of positivity• The further one is removed from the Light, the closer one is drawn to the power and influence of negativity.

10

BINDING BY STRIKING

THIS WAS THE FIRST PARADOX AND THE ROOT of every paradox in the universe. Light emanates to this phase, Malkhut, in response to man's desire, but when that Light arrives it is deflected by the Curtain. Light so repelled is called Returning Light which is said to bind with the Upper Light, giving Illumination to the Upper Emanations. Hence the term, Binding by Striking. The result of this enigmatic phenomenon becomes doubly paradoxical when it is taken into account that this rejection, or casting off, of the Light from this the fourth phase, is the sole means by which the Light becomes manifest.

Positive and negative forces can never be reconciled without the aid of an intermediary. Each tendency remains functional in its own respective state until a bridge is made between them. Just as the filament has the potential ability to create a connection between the positive and negative poles of the lightbulb, so too can man act as a filament between himself and the Light of Creation. It is only through man's conscious restriction, which is tantamount to a personal Tsimtsum, that the Light finds full expression.

The Upper Worlds receive their total illumination, not from the Source, the *Or En Sof,* directly, but as a result of this paradox called Binding by Striking. This concept will receive a more detailed analysis in a later chapter. In the meantime, allow the images of the filament of a lightbulb and the flint in a lighter, both which illuminate through this process of refusal, to stand as reminders of Binding by Striking. In neither instance would the light be revealed were it not for these elements, the filament and the flint, acting contrary to their natural Desire to Receive.

Only man has the free will to exercise the third dimension which is rejection. Man, and man alone, can act as a filament between the *Or En Sof* , the Light of the Endless, and the Encircling Vessels which are within us and all around us, striving for revealment. By his rejection, man duplicates the act of Tsimtsum and thereby creates an affinity, or "similarity of form" with the Light. This is the bridge by which the empty Circular Vessels of man's existence are slowly, yet irrevocably, linked with the Endless Light of Creation.

The Light's sole purpose is to share, but the Vessel's Bread of Shame, which was the cause of the first restriction (Tsimtsum) prevents it from receiving the Light of the Endless without first having earned it. Remember, it was the Vessel that asked to share in the give-and-take of Creation, so that it could be absolved of Bread of Shame, but the Emanator, in granting that wish, created, of necessity, a dissimilarity of form between the Light and the Vessel — for the finite cannot exist in the realm of the Infinite. This situation preordained a condition in which the Vessel would forever be destined to repeat the act of Tsimtsum in order that the mutually exclusive tendencies of the Light, which is to share, and that of the Vessel, which is to receive, can both be satisfied.

A person's encircling vessels receive only the Light which they have the capacity to reveal. The Light never says no, that is man's prerogative and his alone. The paradox lies in the fact that while a man may want to accept the Light which is freely offered he cannot do so without deactivating Bread of Shame. A man can bind or reveal the Light to the upper reaches of his being only by striking the Light away. For if he were to receive the Light directly from the Source, the *Or En Sof*, neither the purpose of the Light nor that of the Vessel would be served. The Light would envelop the Vessel and the universe would revert to a circular condition which would be contrary to the desire of the Vessel whose Bread of Shame originally caused the Light and the Vessel to separate.

From the moment of the Tsimtsum it became the universal condition that the Encircling Vessels, which are the hidden animus of all things on this phase of existence, could never again receive Illumination directly from the *Or En Sof*, but would have to be manifested via man's restrictive capacity. Thus the Curtain, and its effect, that of Binding by Striking, became, and remains, the sole means by which we, the emanated, can reveal the Light that is our essence.

THE CIRCULAR CONCEPT

Some people are connected with the *Or En Sof,* others are not. The difference is affinity. Those who wish to live in a circular context with the Endless may do so by creating an affinity with the Light. Affinity is a circular concept. The Light cannot reveal the Encircling Vessels, which are the essence of man and the universe, unless the Vessel desires revealment.

Through the limited creative process of the Line, a person can reveal the *Or En Sof* , that surrounds him, and at the same time, awaken the *Or En Sof,* the Encircling Vessels, within. The Circle can connect with the Line only when and if he Line makes the connection. We are the Line and only we can link our Inner Light with the Circle of the Endless. Through desire to share we create affinity, through affinity we reveal the Light.

Desire to Receive, as the reader is by now quite well aware, has two aspects, one is to share, the other one is to receive for oneself alone. A person possessed by the latter can never know the Light. However, much Light he may attract is repelled by the Curtain of his negativity. Conversely, the person who seeks Light for the Sake of Sharing, creates an affinity with the Light by living within a circular context, and can therefore,draw Light in direct accordance with his or her needs.

11

INTENTIONS

THE FINAL PRODUCT OF ANY THOUGHT OR action is a direct result of the intention which first gave it impetus. Intentions, like seeds, contain within them all the potential for the roots, branches, leaves, and blossoms of the tree. A well conceived intention results in a well constructed object. The stronger the original intention, the more completely will the final result be manifested.

The same holds true in the physical world as well as in the realm of thoughts, words, and ideas. Make no mistake: Thoughts are things. so too are words, letters, numbers, and ideas. Just as surely as a chair is a thing, 50 too is a prayer, and so too, it logically follows, is an intention. It matters not in which realm of existence one seeks to make his mark, he must begin with an intention.

An intention is like a form, or mold, into which the

cement of creation can be poured. Every thought, word, act, deed, and gesture begins with an intention, known or unknown, conscious or unconscious. Does it not stand to reason that the Creator had an intention when He decided to withdraw the Infinite and thus impart to his creatures love and happiness?

It was with a single Intention that the world began.

ON BECOMING CIRCLE

In Kabbalistic terminology, that which encircles, is that which causes, so when it is written that, 1The Circle of the first emanation was encircled by the Light of the Endless," it means that the first emanation was caused by the Light of the *En Sof*. On a personal level, we find that man is born with inner Encircling Vessels, which, though in a potential state, are capable of manifesting Light. It is possible to bridge the gap between the *Or En Sof* and the potential Encircling Vessels by establishing what is known to Kabbalah as a Circular Concept, meaning that The Desire to Receive for the Sake of Sharing outweighs The Desire to Receive for Oneself Alone.

The Light exists within us and without us, it is a part of us and yet apart from us at the same time. The Or En So/ encircling us (Surrounding Light) exists only for the sake of Sharing. The Inner Light, which is functional in a potential state, is capable of manifesting Surrounding Light, but only when acted upon by the limited creative process, the Line. The Line is man's only link with the *Or En Sof*: It is the filament by which Surrounding Light can fill his inner Encircling Vessels, and thereby reveal through illumination his true, primal nature.

The degree to which we fill our Encircling Vessels depends entirely on the capacity of our filament which is Desire. There is no legal ordinance stating that we have to live within a circular context. Or, if such a law exists, there is no police force, no body politic or inner dynamic, whose duty it is to uphold that law. There is no coercion in spirituality. The light demands nothing from the Vessel. It is the degree to which the Vessel desires that is the sole determining factor in the manifestation of the Light.

The reasons for striving to live within a circular context are myriad. By linking our interi*Or En Sof* with the exteri*Or En Sof*, we establish communication with the source of all things. This Source, the *Or En Sof*, exists in all phases of time-space, energy-matter, cause-effect. By creat-ing a circular concept with the Light, we can "patch in" to the great universal net-work in which each phase, each atom and subatomic speck, is in constant and instant com-munication with every other speck.

The more connections the kabbalist makes between his Inner Light and the Surrounding Light, the more readily can he utilize the all-pervasive universal system. The stronger is his desire to share, the greater is his power to reveal the Light of Creation.

INNER LIGHT - SURROUNDING LIGHT

Rabbi Ashlag's interpretation of the Ari's discourse on Inner Light begins as follows: "In each Sefira we distinguish two types of light: Inner Light and Surrounding Light...."

Inner Light does not illuminate the fourth phase. If it did there could be no diversity of phase between the Light and the Vessel, for the Light would most certainly nullify the Vessel's inherent negativity by drowning it, so to speak, in the immensity of its positive cosmic energy. This Vessel, Malkhut, the fourth phase, must therefore receive Light "at a distance" in the form of Surrounding Light which encircles everything on this planet, in all of its phases.

Just as the ozone layer of the atmosphere repels much of the light that attempts to penetrate it, so too does the Curtain of Malkhut repel the Light of Creation, allowing to enter only that Light which is specifically required. The harmful sunlight, the infrared and ultraviolet, is for the most part repelled, for if it were not rejected it would surely nullify all that is alive on this planet. And as every physical law and manifestation has a metaphysical counterpart, it follows that there must also be a cosmic perimeter which blocks out much of the Light of Creation. In kabbalistic terminology the Restriction and the Curtain on the fourth phase establishes a "Boundary" which limits the extension of the Light to the fourth phase. The total Light received by Malkhut, not including that which was expelled by the Curtain and restriction, is termed, "Limit."

The Earth, and all her creatures, with the sole exception of man, has a built-in limiting mechanism. Man and man alone must consciously restrict his input, for it is only by exacting finitude on the Infinite — in other words, by creating a bridge or filament between the Line and the Circle — that the Encircling Vessels that are within him can again be filled.

It is the purpose of Light to be revealed, and the purpose of man to reveal it. The aura of Surrounding Light encircles every atom in the universe, yet it must remain in a potential state until man by his conscious desire makes the necessary connection which allows the Light to manifest. By our restriction, our denial, we act as a filament which brings forth the light. In this way we fulfill the purpose of both Light and Vessel, Circle and Line: By denying the darkness we reveal the Light, by restricting the negative we release the positive, and in this manner do we absolve the Bread of Shame.

12

THE ESSENCE OF TIME

WORDS LIKE "SOONER," "LATER," "NOW", AND "simultaneous," are relative expressions. What is here and now for one, is there and then for another. From the perspective of a man who is late for an important appointment, time is rushing by at a breakneck pace, while from the point of view of another man who is early for the same appointment, the same time may be dragging by interminably. How time is perceived depends on the perspective from which it is observed.

If the man who is late for the appointment were to be suddenly teleported to his destination, time would immediately be transformed from an angry tyrant into a benign servant, worthy of accolades instead of diatribes for having brought all of the parties together at the same time, in the same place, for the same meeting. Distance (space) plays a part in how we perceive time.

Time, as an entity apart from the space-time continuum, does not exist. Just as height cannot exist without width, and depth cannot exist without the other two linear dimensions, neither can time and space exist independently. Space and time are inseparable. The clock is a man made construct. There is no great clock from which the universe sets its cosmic watch. Nature moves according to the dictates of her own internal, eternal, yet ever-changing, rhythms. Only man marches in time to the beat of a clock. Man, and only man, worships at the altar of time.

While it is true that we cannot stem the tide of the space-time continuum, we can change our perception of it and by so doing significantly alter the course of our lives. Imagine time as a river which runs from the far distant past into the far distant future. Imagine that the now of the river is controlled by your wants and needs, moods and emotions. When your thoughts are clear, so are the waters of time. When you are "agitated" the waters are also agitated. When you are in a hurry (as was the man who was late for his appointment) the banks of the river are narrow and the waters are white-capped rapids. When you are at rest the waters run cool and calm. When you are afraid the waters are dark and ominous. When you are at peace the waters are mirror-glass smooth.

What, then, is the essence of time? Is it a friend or an enemy? Is it our servant, a mere convenience by which we measure our lives, or is it a tyrant who rules over us with an iron hand? Do we use it or does it use us? There is no single answer. In the final analysis time is what you make it.

13

ENERGY-INTELLIGENCE

AT FIRST GLANCE THE ABOVE TWO WORDS may seem mutually exclusive, but from a kabbalistic frame of reference they make perfect sense, for without one the other could not exist. Everything has intelligence. Everything is imbued with the Light of Creation. Everything has the potential to influence for good and for bad. Everything requires a Vessel, and Energy is the Vessel that reveals the Light of Intelligence.

Energy-intelligence is what makes man do what he does: The energy-intelligence called the sefirot of the Desire to Receive of Malkhut, the strongest Desire to Receive. A sefira is a vessel. A vessel is that which reveals. An intelligence must work to reveal.

What makes a rock a rock? As we learned earlier, matter is, if you will, a matter of degree. The Rock of Gibraltar, if it could somehow be compressed into a state devoid of space and atoms, would fit comfortably into a wheelbarrow. The one percent of that rock that gives it shape is that rock's energy-intelligence. The other ninety-nine percent is totally oblivious to the shape of that rock and would just as soon be occupying space in a Manhattan office building, a human being, or a tree.

Energy-intelligence is manifested according to the degree of the Desire to Receive. The greater the Desire to Receive of the Vessel, the greater will be the manifestation of the Light. Inanimate objects have a lesser Desire to Receive than animate life-forms, but all are infused with Intelligence to a lesser or greater degree.

Scientists now tell us of what kabbalists have known for centuries: Everything is connected. There is no space in metaphysics, no time as we know it. We are all a part of some grand space-time-mass-energy spectrum, and within every color of that spectrum from the darkest color to the lightest, lives the potential for influence and communication, give and take. When one energy-intelligence meets another there is potential for attraction or repulsion, collision or merger. When energy-intelligences attract there is said to be an affinity between them. It is this meeting of the minds, if you will, that compels one to pick up a certain rock on a beach instead of a million others. It is the energy-intelligence of two people that attracts them to, or repels them from, each other.

Is a rock a living thing?

Yes, but again it is a matter of degree. A rock has a Desire to Receive, but nowhere near as great as that of a man. As you move up the scale of life through the mineral, vegetal, and animal kingdoms you find a greater Desire to Receive. Still, as small as the Energy-Intelligence of a rock may be, it can still influence, cause a stirring, in the energy-intelligence of a man, if the man is susceptible. A Desire to Receive for oneself alone can make a person susceptible to the negative influences inherent in the energy-intelligence of that rock. Conversely, a strong Desire to Receive so that one may impart can allow a person to come under more positive influences, or not be influenced at all, depending on the best interests of the person involved.

If anyone has trouble believing that a rock can influence a man, consider the men and women who have died while climbing Mount Everest. Why do men climb mountains? The standard answer is, "Because it's there..." The kabbalist would answer, "Because my energy-intelligence has an affinity with its energy-intelligence." In effect, they are two ways of saying the same thing. Many a climber has talked with a mountain, and many a mountain has answered, it is just that the climber has no words to describe the experience so he must rely on the standard reply.

Still not convinced? Consider that our literature, films, and television are filled with wild-eyed men and women who have succumbed to the negative influences of the energy-intelligences of diamonds, gold, and precious stones. Remember the thousands of lives lost in the gold rushes to San Francisco and the Klondike. Men have killed for a single stone; others have served half of their lives in prisons.

Ask them why they did it and they will probably answer, "Because it was there."

THE SOURCE REIGNS SUPREME

The kabbalist seeks to return to the seed of his existence, the source of his stream. The seed contains, in potential form, all of the attributes of the four emanations which have yet to manifest. From the source of the stream of life, the kabbalist gazes on a vista which encompasses past, present, and future — the beginning, the middle, and the end. If he chooses to view the stream from the perspective of the first emanation (Wisdom) the view is not as clear, and from the perspective of the second emanation (Intelligence) the view is dimmer still, and so on down to Malkhut, this world, where the *Or En Sof* is completely obscured by negativity.

For the kabbalist, reality, as defined by worldly standards, is unreality, and the real reality, the first cause, the source, the *Or En Sof*, lies one phase beyond. By connecting with the Endless, the kabbalist fills his inner Encircling Vessels, thereby creating a similarity of form between himself and the worlds around him, which in turn sheds Light on every phase of his life. By bridging the gap with the Light around him, he reveals the Light within.

A WORLD APART

Although Keter (Crown), the first stage in any manifestation, embodies the potential for all stages of a manifestation, it is not included in the chain of events through which all things must pass in order to find full expression. The line must act upon the circle. Desire gives expression to the Light. *The En Sof,* the Keter of Everything, has no need to become manifested on a physical level. It is we who give It expression. By our prayers we give It expression, by our thoughts, both positive and negative, by our words, and by our deeds.

A seed, the Keter of a tree, would never grow in a vacuum-sealed container. Certain conditions must be satisfied before the seed's potential can be realized, and until those conditions are addressed the seed will remain in the Circular phase of its existence: Having no desire to grow, it does not grow. This is one example of why the Keter, in this case the seed, is not considered a part of the process that leads to manifestation.

The brain, the Keter of a man, registers every pain and tactile impulse in the body, and yet it remains blissfully ignorant of its own pain and discomfort. Consider the ease with which we can "read" the character or intentions of another person, and the difficulty we have in coming to know ourselves. The brain we have, it seems, plays the leading role in the drama which is our lives, but only if it is acted upon by outside influences which are brought about as a result of Desire.

SMOKING IS HAZARDOUS TO YOUR HEALTH

Why do we succumb to evil? What is the nature of temptation? Why will some men give up their loved ones and families and even their lives in pursuit of ill gotten gains? We know that smoking, drugs, and alcohol pose serious dangers to our health, and yet we go on using them. Why?

As mentioned earlier, the negative aspect of any energy-intelligence has the potential to influence any other, but only if one allows itself to be susceptible to the other. All of us, in other words, are subject to negativity, but only some of us fall under its influence.

Why are some of us seemingly impervious to the effects of these evil influences while others seem endlessly to be caught up in their clutches?

To learn the answer we must go back to the *En Sof* before the restriction when the souls of man asked to share in the give and take of Creation. When the Light granted free will to the Vessel it gave up some of its power so that the Vessel would be allowed to express its Desire to Receive. The Light withdrew, in other words, so that Darkness could have expression. In this way did the Creator allow evil Klippot (Shells of Husks) to encircle both Himself and His creations.

Man allows evil. A man who connects only with the external, a man whose Desire to Receive for Himself Alone outweighs his Desire to Receive for the Sake of Imparting, falls easy prey to the influence of negativity; whereas the man who connects with the internal, a man whose desires are in proper balance with the wants and needs of others, is much less susceptible to the influence of negativity and the temptations constantly posed by evil.

14

BREAD OF SHAME

ONE OF THE MOST PERVASIVE OF ALL HUMAN traits is guilt. Like fear, guilt produces a magnification of the senses, but unlike fear, which usually incapacitates temporarily — as with a fright of short duration — guilt can be protracted over a significant portion of a person's lifespan. Yet, in the end, no matter how hard the guilty party works to cover the tracks of his or her indiscretions, the truth invariably comes to Light.

To live in a world of guilt is to live in a world of distortion. The guilty man must watch his every move. Fear of discovery lurks in the darkened corners of his imagination. Small becomes large, large becomes larger. The world seems out of proportion. For him the walls have ears. Even a casual comment can send the guilty party into a fit of paranoia. An innocent remark made by another in jest, might, for the guilty one, carry heavy portent: News as to how far his guilt has traveled, a clue as to the traitor who might have revealed his unconscionable deed.

Intense self-scrutiny, such as is engaged in by those whose normal reactions are paralyzed by guilt, causes acute self-consciousness which compels the guilty party to invent an increasingly elaborate network of feints and fabrications in order to explain away his unusual behavior. In time it becomes impossible to hold up the flimsy foundation of pretenses on which the guilty party has constructed his edifice of lies. He grows weary, depleted of psychic and physical energy. No longer can he abide the need for disguises, no longer can he maintain the charade which has become his life. Like a spider caught in a web of its own creation, the guilty man struggles vainly to escape the net of his illusions, until, at last, the intricate structure, so painstakingly woven from the sticky stuff of lies, closes around him — a predicament from which there is ultimately only one escape: The truth.

RESTRICTION

Early Man devised a method by which to start a fire that consisted of striking a hard rock against a softer rock with the intention of producing sparks. A similar restrictive action, known to Kabbalah as Binding by Striking, must take place in every instance where Light is brought into this world. A contraction must take place, a Tsimtsum, so that Light may be revealed.

Revealment begins with restriction.

A woman's uterine contractions precede the miracle of birth. Athletes, and also body builders, have an expression, "Pain is Gain" which attests to the exact correlation of results produced with the degree of restriction imposed upon the musculature. Even on a metaphysical or thought level we see that the same principle is valid. Concentration, narrowing (restricting) the focus of our thoughts is necessary in order to manifest words and ideas of the highest order. Where little restriction is exercised the thoughts produced are of the "like, well... you know" variety.

The more resistance a filament is capable of producing, the greater is the revealment of Light. The restrictive capacity of the filament in a light bulb, the flint in a lighter, or what we will call the life-force of a human being, wears down eventually making it impossible for the Vessel to reveal the universal energy-intelligence, Light.

Of all the creatures on this world the human being alone lacks an instinctive restrictive mechanism. Before the Tsimtsum, you will remember, we asked for and received a degree of free will which allows us to reveal the Light or not, as we so desire. Either we must consciously re-enact the Tsimtsum and in so doing absolve Bread of Shame, or succumb to negativity and remain in darkness. Light never diminishes, only the capacity for restriction.

By our conscious restriction we reveal the Light. If we choose not to restrict we allow for the existence of darkness. By restriction we eliminate Bread of Shame, while not exercising restriction imprisons us in a state of psychological, emotional, and spiritual unfulfillment. When viewed from this kabbalistic perspective the choice presented to humanity on this phase of existence boils down to one absurdly simple solution:

Restrict so that the Light may be revealed.

TSIMTSUM

The Restriction created the illusion of darkness. Concealed though It may be, the Light still provides the impetus for our every thought and action. The impressions implanted in the Encircling Sefirot will allow us no rest, no peace, no contentment, until the Light has been revealed anew. The Ari, Rabbi Isaac Luria, of blessed memory, taught us that the one true purpose of existence is to restore Light, as much as is humanly possible, to its original, circular, Infinite condition through the limited creative process of the Line.

We falsely believe that our restless search for satisfaction will one day result in the fulfillment of our desires, but in reality we already possess everything that will bring us true and lasting satisfaction. Deluged as we are by an endless stream of sensory stimulation, one might easily be deceived into thinking that the world of appearances, the world we see, hear, taste, touch, and smell, is the be all and end all of existence. That is why the kabbalist seeks not to satisfy the myriad superficial desires presented by the world of illusion, but to restrict them — for by so doing he or she ignites, through the act of Binding by Striking, the Infinite Light of Creation and thereby absolves Bread of Shame.

Yet, logically we cannot go back in time to the *En Sof* before the Thought of Creation — or can we?

The Tsimtsum that catapulted us from Infinity into creation was only the first of untold billions of tsimtsums that were to follow. Countless tsimtsums take place every second. Stopping a car, turning off the ignition, locking the door, switching off a light, closing out a bank account, shutting one's eyes to go to sleep, all are tsimtsums. Every time we say no and really mean it we re-enact Tsimtsum.

The kabbalist resists that which would take him from his mission to restore the Light. He repels temptation, obstructs deception, denies illusion; he restricts pride and vanity, resists fraud and duplicity. He narrows his frame of reference to the root cause, the primal essence of existence, for only from the perspective of the source can all future emanations be seen.

To focus is to restrict, to restrict is to create affinity with the Creator. The longer and more attentively we restrict our focus to the physical or metaphysical manifestation on which our sites are set, the greater is the probability of successful completion. By consciously re-enacting the Tsimtsum process we rekindle the ancient spark of Infinity.

THE OFFSPRING OF RESTRICTION

The Ari, Rabbi Isaac Luria, described the Curtain in Kabbalah — "Ten Luminous Emanations" as being the "Power of Restriction" which is awakened when the Light reaches the fourth phase, "...striking and pushing the Light backwards." Curtain is the power which prevents Light from spreading to the fourth phase. It is not the restriction of Tsimtsum per se, but a further restriction which only happens at. the moment when the Light of Creation reaches this, the fourth phase. In other words, when Tsimtsum acts involuntarily to repel the Light of the Infinite it is called Mesech, or Curtain.

The Sefirot of Straightness, acting in conjunction with the power which is the Curtain, represents a paradox in that both behave in complete opposition to their natural Desire to Receive. In this sense, the Curtain has much in common with the filament of a lightbulb which also acts contrary to its natural inclination. The light which manifests inside a lightbulb is not, as most people imagine, the result of some harmonious conversion of electricity within the filament. Rather it is the effect produced by a violent resistance, or throwing off, restricting the negative pole — the natural inclination of which is the Desire to Receive. This action known as Binding by Striking, might be likened to a person who asks another for a gift, but when that gift is given the receiver throws it back into the benefactor's face. The negative pole, in effect, is asking the positive pole for electricity, and the positive pole, whose desire is to impart, readily complies. Which brings us to the paradox: Instead of accepting the electricity it just asked for, the negative pole repels it, thereby causing the filament to heat up to red hot intensity and the light to be revealed. In human terms, on a physical level, the involuntary narrowing of the eyes when we walk from darkness into strong light, is the Curtain, and such is its contrary, though absolutely essential, nature.

The Curtain, then, represents a duality of purpose and function in that it contains both a quality of restriction and a quality of reconciliation. While it protects us from the Light, at the same time it denies us access to it. What need have we for protection from the *Or En Sof* which is, after all, a part of us? Just as the eyes must adjust to changes in light, so too must the "eyes" of the soul be prepared before gazing on the Light of the Endless. Just as a lightbulb would be obliterated by the sudden infusion of a million watts of raw electric power, so too would an unwary life-force be vaporized by direct connection with the *Or En Sof*.

Pause to consider the unimaginable power that is contained within each of us. The most famous formula in the modern world, $E=mc2$, expresses this power vividly. Simply stated it means that the "bottled-up" energy contained in any piece of matter is equal to the mass of that piece of matter times the astronomical number of the speed of light (186,000 miles per second) squared! What this means, hypothetically, is that a sudden release of the energy held captive within a single strand of hair would produce an explosion of such magnitude as to be felt around the world. Is it any wonder that we need protection from the *Or En Sof*?

Conversely, any denial of the Light of Creation, as represented by the Curtain, whether involuntary or not, is a negation of both the Light and the Vessel. The Curtain negates the Light by denying its true purpose which is to share, and it also denies the Light access to the Vessel whose desire is to receive. Thus does the Curtain prevent both Light and Vessel from living up to their true potential.

If the Creator is all-powerful why does He allow the Curtain to shut Him out?

To answer that question we must go back to the *En Sof* before the Thought of Creation. The Vessel asked for the right to share in the give and take of Creation and the Light, whose sole purpose in creating the emanated beings was to impart peace and happiness to them, granted that wish. The Creator then had to withdraw, for no negativity could exist as a separate entity in the light of creation, just as no darkness can exist in a place where there is strong light. And so the Creator consciously limited his power in order that we, the emanated, could be granted free will, and therefore it is incumbent upon us to purify the selfish desire wherein lies the Curtain in order that we may complete the cycle of imparting and receiving.

How can this be accomplished?

In the words of the Ari, "...the surrounding Light then exerts itself to purify the Curtain, according to whatever the amount of longing there is." Longing, of course, is synonymous with desire. The negative energy which is the Curtain can be purified, but only if there is great longing on the part of the Vessel (soul) to receive the Light for the sake of sharing.

And here again the paradox surfaces: By negating the negative we release the positive and move closer to the Endless Circle of Creation.

15

CURTAINS

THERE ARE TWO MODES OF RESTRICTION, Tsimtsum and the Curtain. The first is voluntary, the second, involuntary. Either we restrict our Desire to Receive for Ourselves Alone, meaning we create affinity with the Light by repeating Tsimtsum, or restriction will occur regardless through the activation of the Curtain. This situation was of our own making. The Tsimtsum resulted from our desire to be released from the burden of Bread of Shame, and because of that restriction we can no longer receive anything in good conscience that has not been earned.

The thief is an embodiment of Desire to Receive for oneself alone. While he may imagine himself in some romantic context the thief is really in a *Catch-22* situation. No joy can he receive from that which he steals unless and until he has dealt with Bread of Shame. Generally a thief will do this in one of two ways. Either he consciously lifts Bread of Shame by spending like the proverbial drunken sailor, or, if he is a more experienced thief who has tired of the cycle of fortunes slipping through his fingers, he invests his money wisely, lays low, lives frugally, and then makes some minor "mistake" while in the middle of one of his ventures such as leaving a single fingerprint on a window or a doorknob which allows him to correct his behavior in a federal prison. And so it goes, around and around on an endless treadmill of unfulfillment.

Of the two methods used by thieves to absolve Bread of Shame, the former is a case of voluntary restriction (Tsimtsum), in that no one coerces him into throwing away his money — he makes a conscious decision to "live for today." The latter is an example of involuntary restriction, for even though the frugal thief "tsimtsums" initially, insofar as he restricts himself from throwing his money away — the Curtain descends upon him anyway because he has not dealt with Bread of Shame. Those few thieves who steal and never get caught alleviate Bread of Shame through other means such as living in cells of their own making, prisons of paranoia and self-induced solitary confinement. Never does the thief find anything but transitory pleasure from that which he has stolen. In spite of all his attempts to convert his spoils into some type of lasting satisfaction he can never truly enjoy his ill-gotten treasures because the energy-intelligence of those goods belongs to someone else. He may "launder" the money, but that in itself will never cleanse his dirty conscience.

Habitual thievery is by no means the only negative activity subject to the paradox. Compulsive behavior of any kind is an indication of Desire to Receive for Oneself Alone. Eating, drinking, smoking, drug taking, working, and sexual compulsiveness, all have the potential to provoke similar outcomes in terms of the two kinds of restriction. Either the smoker voluntarily restricts his intake of smoke (Tsimtsum) or emphysema, or some other involuntary ailment (Curtain), will do it for him. The overeater can consciously restrain his appetite (Tsimtsum) or an involuntary Curtain of high blood pressure or cholesterol will create a life-threatening situation. The alcoholic either stops drinking or his liver gives out. The workaholic consciously restricts his hours or a heart attack does it for him. And so on. If any habituated individual does not learn to consciously restrict his indulgence of that to which he is addicted, it will, to use an old expression, be "curtains" for him.

It is truly ironic that by consciously rejecting that which we think we want we reveal what we really want — not the avaricious longings of our bodies, or the minor matters that are important to our "rational" minds, but the true and lasting desire of our inner encircling vessels which is to reveal the Light within.

16

SYMMETRY

AN ASPECT OF THE GRAND REFORMATION that unfolded after the Tsimtsum was the emergences of five worlds. These worlds, listed in relation to their proximity to the Infinite, from the highest to the lowest are:

· 1. Primordial Man — Archetypal
2. The World of Emanation
3. The World of Creation
4. The World of Formation
5. The World of Action

When the Creator withdrew to make room for free will and the Desire to Receive, the circular condition became linear, hence the concept of limitation. The Creator gave us the choice to manifest Energy according to our Desire to Receive. The Creator imposed a limitation on Himself (Tsimtsum) and from that

moment on the vessel could receive Light or not according to its own free will. We are the Vessel. It is we who must choose whether or not to manifest the Light of Creation.

From the kabbalistic perspective, the Line is Adam. Both represent the first limitation. Here, for the first time, the souls of man which had previously been an undifferentiated aspect of a circular (Infinite) condition now became linear or finite. No longer were the souls of man an unexpressed aspect of the endless wheel of Creation. Now, the pure spirit that was man would be housed in a body whose life was finite, having a beginning, a middle, and an end. Like the veils covering the ten divine Sefirothic Vessels, henceforth would the souls of man be clothed in flesh and encircled by Klippot.

CONCENTRIC CIRCLES OF UNDERSTANDING

When we speak of a Vessel without a Curtain we use the term Circle. Negativity can cloud our actions and reactions. A person who is not "weighed down" by husks or shells of negativity (Klippot) is closer to the Infinite, and hence deemed higher, than one who is encumbered by the weight of negative thoughts and emotions. A "circular concept" is defined as: "The balance between left and right, negative and positive, brought about by the use of restriction." Only man has the option of exercising free will when it comes to his. own spiritual evolvement. The closer one becomes with the endless circle of Creation, the less encumbered one is by negativity, the closer one is to creating a circular concept with himself and the world around him.

A man caught up in his own desires is like a snake eating its own tail. The Desire to Receive for Oneself Alone causes layer upon layer of negativity to build up around a person — the greater the Desire to Receive, the greater is the constriction. Farther and farther does he recede from the circular concept, blinder and blinder does he become to the Light of Creation, until, at last, the connection with the *Or En Sof* has been completely severed. Thus, with blinded eyes, he goes through life unaware that the brilliant, endless Light of *En Sof* is within him, and all around him, and could be his for the asking.

By transforming our Desire to Receive for ourselves alone into a Desire to Receive for the sake of Imparting we can break the chains of negativity that imprison us. Only by re-creating an affinity with the *Or En Sof* can we fill the Encircling Vessel within us all. How can we lift the veils of our own negativity and rise to our fullest potential? Shakespeare wrote that the world is a stage. Yes, it is a stage — this physical world, Malkhut, is a stage of spiritual development, and only by creating a circular concept can we raise the Curtain of negativity that surrounds us to meld with the circular Light of Creation.

SYMMETRY

An understanding of the nature of symmetry is essential to a proper understanding of Kabbalah. In fact, it may be said that to comprehend symmetry is to comprehend the very workings of Nature itself. Everything strives toward symmetry. Negative seeks positive; cause seeks effect; darkness seeks light. Or, to cite a kabbalistic frame of reference: The Light, *The*

Desire to Impart, seeks The Vessel, *The Desire to Receive.*

Physicists now believe that all natural forces exist solely to allow nature to maintain an abstract balanced symmetry. This constant striving toward equilibrium, in Oriental philosophy, is known as the Male-Female principle, Yang and Yin. Mystics dubbed it simply, life-force. From a Kabbalistic point of view, the spirit-body spectrum is one in which energy, or spirit, is connected with the Light, or Life-giving entity, while the body is the material expression of the energy which results from a melding of the two.

One needs only look into a full-length mirror for a practical demonstration of symmetry at work: Two arms, two hands, two legs, two feet, two ears, two nostrils, two of almost everything. Even our brain is divided into two distinct parts which are often at odds with each other and constantly seeking equilibrium. Scientists have discovered that the left half of your brain operates at a much higher speed than the right. Hence, in order to achieve a balanced mental state it is necessary for either the right side to speed up (which can be accomplished through some forms of dance, music, and active meditation, or, to a lesser and inferior extent through the use of intoxicants) or for the left side to slow down, which is achieved through passive meditation and deep relaxation. This constant striving toward symmetry affects every aspect of our lives. When we are out of balance mentally, emotionally, or physically, an instinctual reflex seeks to balance the scales again.So to understand the dynamics of balance is to understand the nature of life itself. We live in a world of perpetual correction and Kabbalah teaches us how to achieve what is perhaps the only type of equilibrium of which man is or will ever be capable, the symmetry which is achieved by cleaving with the Infinite.

17

The Primordial Man

IN THE PREVIOUS CHAPTER, REFERENCE WAS made to recent developments in split-brain research, pointing to the fact that the left cerebral hemisphere operates much faster than the right. Many of us are by now familiar with the characteristic attributes of the right and left hemispheres, the left being in control of language and the more cognitive and scientific skills, while the right houses the more artistic side of our temperament.

Another division should also be noted, the division between the front brain, or cerebrum which is the center of our reasoning faculties, and the back brain, or cerebellum, which is the principal organ of the central nervous system. It is said that the cerebrum contains the newest, most human, circuitry, while the cerebellum is comprised of circuits which were patterned in primordial times.

The human brain, then, has four distinct divisions and not two as is commonly believed, and these four divisions concur and coincide completely with the four phases described in the Kabbalah and indeed with the entire Sefirothic system. And it also confirms the Kabbalistic contention that man is a universe unto himself, with the history of the world, past, present, and future, etched into his circuitry.

That may seem like a tenuous leap of logic to some, until they examine more closely the make-up of the human brain. Consider that our skulls contain an old brain and a new brain. Within the old brain are two brains, an old reptilian brain that was perfected 200 to 300 million years ago and is identical to that of a lizard, and an old mammalian brain that is nearly as ancient. Consider too that the very chemicals and compounds of which our bodies are composed are only the most recent metamorphosis of materials that have been around since the beginning of time and will be here long after time, as we currently keep track of it, has been forgotten.

We are all models of the universe, encyclopedias, living museums of all that is, was, or ever will be.

THE EMERGENCE OF THE CENTRAL COLUMN

Before the universe became the multiverse that we live in today, there were only two inherent aspects in nature. Kabbalah describes them as Light and Vessel. Ancient Oriental cosmogony calls these two opposing, though complementary, forces the Male-Female Principle, or Yang and Yin. Like Light in the Kabbalistic lexicon, Yang represents the male-creative aspect, while Yin, synonymous with the Kabbalistic, Vessel, represents the female-receptive of existence. Everything in the world was, and is, endowed with both Light and Vessel attributes in varying degrees. The following chart will provide the student of Kabbalah with practical demonstration of how the principle of Light and Vessel applied to the physical world.

Many more examples could be given, but it is hoped that these few will help the student better understand the concept of Light and Vessel and just how myriad and all encompassing are their implications. According to adherents of the so-called New Physics, the purpose of nature, all action and reaction in the universe, is a striving towards an abstract symmetry. When this "new" and "futuristic" theory is finally proven, science will again be confirming what has been common knowledge to kabbalists for thousands of years.

On an atomic level, hydrogen, the most abundant element in the universe represents a pure example of Light and Vessel. As hydrogen is the only element devoid of a neutron, it alone stands as an example of the world as it was before the emergence of the Central Column. In this sense, it is a throwback to the world of Primordial Man, when there was but a "Single Line" which was composed of Light and Vessel. Only later at a lower level did the forces congeal to form a third energy-intelligence, the mediating principle known to Kabbalah as the Central Column.

This third factor, described atomically as the neutron, displays two tendencies, one of restriction, the other of reconciliation. When the negative energy of the Left Column which is the Desire to Receive is activated, the Central Column acts to restrain

it. The nature of the Central Column is to provide a bridge
between the Right and Left columns, allowing the energy of the
imparting aspect of the Right to make use of the energy of the
Left. Only when all three columns are in balance does the system
operate at peak efficiency.

STRAIGHT FROM THE SOURCE

Straight Light emerges directly from the source without
intervention on the part of the Vessel. That is not to underesti-
mate the Vessel's essential role in the manifestation of Straight
Light. There would be no Illumination in any phase were it not
for Desire to Receive which is an attribute not of Light, but solely
of the Vessel.

It is an ironic twist of metaphysics that Desire to Receive for
Oneself Alone sheds more Illumination on others than it does on
oneself. The negative aspect of Desire emitted by the greedmongers
of this fourth phase makes it possible for them to draw a large quan-
tity of Light, but the klippot ("husks" or "shells" of negativity)
allows no light to enter them. The Light attracted by them is
repelled away from the Curtain of their greed by the action referred
to earlier, namely, the involuntary restriction of the curtain.

Those, on the other hand, who desire Light for the sake of
sharing, are blessed with Light for others and rewarded with Light
with which to permanently illuminate their internal encircling
vessels. And therein lies the irony. Though the desire of the avaricious man may be far stronger than that of the unselfish man, it is
the man whose desire is to share who is the recipient of the
Straight Light inadvertently repelled by the other.

18

STEP BY STEP

WHEN THE ARI, RABBI ISAAC LURIA (1534-1572),
founder of the Lurianic system of Kabbalah, used terms such as
"pure and impure," "slowly and immediately," "thick and thin,"
"ascent and descent," "near and far," "head," "floor," "life," "line,"
and "conclusion," he was conveying meanings for those words and
phrases which were entirely different from their dictionary definitions. The sixteen volumes of Rabbi Ashlag's monumental work,
Kabbalah: "Ten Luminous Emanations", are laced through with
words and references which when happened upon by the uninitiated reader prove baffling at best, but more likely completely
incomprehensible. The reason for this is threefold: On a mundane
level, the Ari's extremely complex thought processes (which were
recorded not by himself but by disciples) have lost something in
their translation from the original Hebrew, and finally into
English. Secondly, at that time it was necessary that the teachings
of Kabbalah, "the soul of the soul of the law," which were passed

on only to the most worthy initiates, remained hidden from oppressive governments and monarchies. By far the most important and telling reason that the Ari's teachings are so difficult to understand for the uninitiated reader, however, is the fact that the Ari, Rabbi Isaac Luria, was attempting to convey with language concepts and meanings for which no words existed. Therefore, he was forced to adapt common words to convey new meanings. Once this is understood the "Ten Luminous Emanations" becomes much easier to comprehend.

With this new information in mind, let us now examine some of the above-mentioned words and phrases, as well as some that have not yet been mentioned, in order that the reader may begin to understand their kabbalistic interpretations. For definitions of the many words and references which have been excluded from this chapter see the section of this book titled, Kabbalistic Terminology.

The Ari stated that: "Light which emerges according to the laws of the four phases, step by step, from pure to thick or impure, then stops at the fourth phase, is called Straight Line."

A detailed analysis of even a single sentence of the Ari's could take a chapter in and of itself. Our intention here, however, is to provide the reader with an overview from which to launch further study. And as it is the purpose of Kabbalah to make internal and emotional connections with the immense power that resides within us all, the reader should allow himself but scant satisfaction at being able to comprehend intellectually these concepts which are reduced to simple terms. The reader should take none of the kabbalistic writings at face value and should always be trying to make the proper metaphysical connections. Read, then, with a certain degree of caution, the following detailed, though greatly simplified, interpretations, keeping in mind the real connection to this material cannot be gleaned merely through the intellect.

LIGHT	VESSEL
Desire to Impart	Desire to Receive
Right Column	Left Column
Light	Darkness
Male	Female
Yang	Yin
Positive	Negative
Sender	Receiver
Proton	Electron
Plus	Minus
Intellect	Intuition
White-reflective	Black- absorbent
Alkaline	Acidic
Hard	Soft
Active-doing	Passive-being
Perfection	Completeness

The first phrase of the sentence reads: "Light which emerges according to the laws of the four phases..." What does this mean? Light, of course, refers to the *Or En Sof*, the Light of the Endless, while, *emerges through the laws of the four phases*, refers to the four stages of Desire to Receive through which all physical manifestations must proceed in their evolvement. They are: 1. Emanation

(Wisdom) 2. Creation (Intelligence) 3. Formation (Beauty — which is further subdivided into Mercy, Judgment, Beauty, Endurance, Majesty, and Foundation) and 4. One Hundred Blessings (Kingdom or Malkhut: This world — physicality).

The latter part of the sentence reads: "...step by step," (meaning through cause and effect), "from pure to the thick or impure..." (obscured from a lesser to a greater degree by negative "shells" known as Klippot) "and then stops at the fourth phase..." (this world) "is called Straight Line." As we learned earlier, the Line is a convenient method by which tO conceptualize finitude. In other words, before the Tsimtsum (restriction) the Light of the *En Sof* was infinite and hence deemed circular, while later, after the Tsimtsum, the Light took on a finite quality which is designated as linear, hence the concept of the Line.

The descent of the Upper Light to the impure vessels of the fourth phase is described as being "straight" because just as the Earth's gravity exerts a direct influence on a falling stone, in a similar manner do the Vessels of Straightness whose longing is strong, cause light to descend "swiftly in a Straight Line." Even the word "swiftly" here means something different from what it seems. By common definition, the word "swiftly" entails the rapid movement of something through time-space. Kabbalistically speaking,

Light does not move at all. Only the vessels move, the quanta, and how can something that does not move, swiftly? Compare the slow meandering of a feather as it falls to the ground, with the straight and swift trajectory of a stone as a means by which to connect with the idea behind the phrase "swiftly in a Straight Line." Straight Illumination is direct and finite. Circular Illumination is Infinite.

Let us now examine another of the Ari's observations on the extension of Light into the void: "When the Light of the Endless was drawn in the form of a straight line in the void, it was not drawn and extended immediately downward, indeed it extended slowly — at first the Line of Light began to extend and at the very start of its extension in the secret of the Line, it was drawn and shaped into a wheel."

Here again the language, if taken at face value, would be most confusing. Words like immediately and slowly refer to time, but as we know, spiritual or holy time has nothing to do with chronological time. Immediately, in this instance means, "without a change of degrees." In other words, the Light Of the *En Sof* was changed very little in the first stage of emanation which is known as Adam Kadmon. The word slowly, on the other hand, means "evolution Of degrees," referring to the four phases, Emanation, Formation, Creation, and Action, which are necessary for existence on a physical level. When the Ari speaks of Light being "drawn" in a straight line, it is possible that the image of a pencil or other writing implement might enter the reader's mind. Of course the Ari was not speaking of drawing a line. Rather, here the word "drawn" is similar to the connotation of that word as it is used in the phrase "drawing water from a well." Desire draws the Light through its phases.

The final segment of the sentence we are analyzing reads: "...the Line of Light began to extend, and at the very start of its extension in the secret of the Line, it was drawn and shaped into a wheel." The word "wheel" refers to a Sefirot of Circles, meaning that very little had changed in the first phase of emanation, Adam Kadmon. The Light still had a connection with the Infinite.

Circular Light reveals no gradations, no "above and below." The four grades of Desire to Receive were present in the world of Adam Kadmon (as they were in the *En Sof* before the restriction), but they were still not as yet individuated. Hence, the Light of the Line is said to have been "dressed in the Circle" a condition designated as "Wheel."

By now the reader is beginning to realize the dangers inherent in a literal interpretation of ancient Kabbalistic texts. This should by no means discourage the reader, for just as it is necessary for a reader of a novel or fantasy to suspend his or her disbelief, it is necessary when studying Kabbalah to suspend the normal, habitual thought processes. The kabbalist goes to great lengths in order that this suspension of ordinary reality may be accomplished. Practices which may seem strange, or even ridiculous, to the casual observer, such as the long (though for the kabbalist, timeless) hours spent assiduously rearranging the four letters of the Holy Name into seemingly countless combinations and permutations, is actually done solely with this transcendent purpose in mind. These practices will be discussed in later volumes.

In an earlier chapter we deliberated briefly upon the emergence of the Central Column. The phase we have been analyzing in this chapter, Adam Kadmon, also known as Primordial Man, was a stage at which the Central Column had not yet become differentiated from the "Single Line" because the Light had yet to be drawn through the four stages necessary for the completion of a Partzuf or complete structure. The third column merged, or perhaps it would be better to say re-emerged, only after the four stages, Light (Wisdom), Water (Intelligence), Firmament (Beauty), and One Hundred Blessings (Kingdom), had been completed and the World of Emanation was born.

The reader should be reminded that while the Ari was imparting to his disciples the kabbalistic interpretation of the beginnings of creation, each and every point that has been mentioned has practical viability here on the physical plane of existence. The process of the four stages discussed in such great detail by Rabbi Luria is much more than just the process through which the universe came into being. It is the process through which everything emerges from the primordial "stew" of creation into physical, conceptual, or even theoretical being. The Ari was discussing the four phases or stages through which anything and everything must pass so as to become manifested. That process never changes. Whether we are discussing the birth of a child, the growth of a tree, the movement of tides or quantum tendencies, or the development from youth to maturity of a human being or any living thing: The process remains the same. The outer manifestations may differ radically, but not the inner process of the four emanations.

The laws of cause and effect — which are equally valid in the metaphysical world — dictate that the process proceed step by step through the four phases. One level must be a complete structure unto itself before the next level can come into existence. Thus, the kabbalist might find himself speaking of the fourth phase of the fourth phase, or the third phase of the second phase. And while to the casual observer this part of Kabbalah may seem complex to the point of unintelligibility, from the perspective of the kabbalist the opposite is true. For by observing the world through the framework of the four phases, all things become intelligible. Instead of getting lost in the millions upon millions of outer manifestations, the kabbalist, by observing but a single process, can understand all things.

19

FREE WILL

THE ARI TAUGHT US: "IT IS IMPOSSIBLE FOR any desire to be stirred up in Existence unless at an earlier time a fulfillment was revealed sufficient to that Desire." This startling revelation might in itself be the subject of a series of volumes. The implications stagger the imagination. It means that material manifestations are more the product of thought than of physical making; that completion precedes fabrication; that every thought, every action, is preceded by an impulse that contains all of the potentialities and possible outcomes; that the carrot follows the donkey; that the cart leads the horse; that the effect is the cause of the cause; that there is no initiative, no free will as that term is generally perceived: It means that the fulfillment precedes the need.

The vessel, man, has no ability to take initiative. All activity begins with a force that wants to be revealed. Not one conscious move is made by any human being without there first being a reason to make that move. One does not scratch an itch unless there is an itch to be scratched. Longing does not manifest of its own accord, there must be something to long for. Desire does not just pop into existence, there must be a need to fulfill before that desire can manifest. The goal must exist before the means to reach that goal comes into existence.

This kabbalistic tenet as been the subject of derision since the advent of modern science. Yet today we see a wave of new scientific theories which echo this principle. Quantum mechanics acknowledges that we, by our intentions, create movement in subatomic particles — thoughts create manifestations in the subatomic world. Botanist Rupert Sheldrake, a former director of biochemistry studies at Cambridge University, has created a series of experiments which strongly suggest that there are "invisible organizing structures that mold or shape things like crystals, plants and animals, and also have an organizing effect on behavior." A complete description of Dr. Sheldrake's radical "new" theory of "morphogenetic fields" would not be appropriate in this volume, but should his theory be proven it would verify what kabbalists have known for centuries: Thoughts and intentions create metaphysical molds into which we can pour the cement of physical manifestation.

Kabbalah is a goal-means system — the goal-means, like space-time, and energy-matter, are inseparable. By knowing the process, by living the process, one can understand the process from beginning to end. The more fully something is established in the mind, the better is the chance for a successful completion. The entire process manifests first in the mind. Even in potential state there must be a completion of the creative process in advance.

Channels exist in nature, but not in man. By initiating the channels we establish the process. Once we have established the channels we know the secret of how to remove the Tsimtsum and Curtain and thereby enhance greatly our chances for creating enduring manifestations which benefit ourselves and all mankind.

PROBING THE NATURE OF INTELLIGENCE

What constitutes intelligence? Is it the capacity to acquire and apply knowledge? The faculty of though and reason? The ability to adapt to new situations? The faculty of perceiving and comprehending meaning? The inherent ability to seize the essential factors of a complex matter? The ability to learn from experience? Mental quickness? Active intellect? Superior powers of the mind?

The answer, of course, is all of the above, and much more. Scientists have identified as many a two hundred different types of intelligence. Still, Science has a long way to go before accepting the kabbalistic definition. Intelligence, kabbalistically speaking, is nothing more nor less than desire, the Desire to Receive. Everything, animate and inanimate, from the lowest order to the highest, is possessed of Desire to Receive to a greater or lesser degree and is therefore also endowed with energy-intelligence.

Why does one child do well in school while another who is as intelligent, or even more so, do poorly? One might answer that the child who does well in school has a better memory than the one who does poorly and is therefore more intelligent. In fact, the opposite is closer to being true. Memory has been proven to be a poor indicator of intelligence. People with excellent memories tend to rely on them to the detriment of their more cognitive and creative abilities. Would not a better explanation be that one child simply has a greater desire to do well in school than the other?

How else, but for desire, can one account for an obvious mathematical genius such as Albert Einstein being seemingly incapable of learning mathematics? Did his brain undergo some miraculous transformation? Did he discover some miraculous diet which helped to strengthen his brain cells? Does it not seem more likely that he had little desire to learn mathematics in his early years and an inordinately strong desire to learn the subject later in his life?

Let us now consider the method by which intelligence is currently measured in our society, IQ tests. Desire, being the kabbalistic criterion for judging intelligence, it would follow that the only reason one person achieves a higher score on an IQ test than another is because that person has either a greater desire to have a higher IQ or has a greater desire to possess the knowledge that will give him or her a higher IQ. In neither case does the higher score indicate true intelligence as IQ examinations measure but a modicum of a person's mental acuity and potential. However much insecurity a high score may alleviate, however self-aggrandizing it may be, in the end a high IQ is the measure of next to nothing.

One has only to attend a meeting of Mensa, or another of the mutual admiration societies for people with high IQ's, to realize that the average genius, as measured solely by scores on IQ examinations, is probably no more intelligent, and probably less interesting than, say, the average man on the street — though it must be admitted that the geniuses can most likely regurgitate more rote-learned facts and information. Consider, as another example, the recent television program which featured four young women with supposed genius IQ's who had posed naked for a men's magazine. What was their reason? Fame? Fortune? No, in all seriousness they stated that they wanted to prove that it is possible for intelligent women to also be beautiful. Certainly, the bodies of these young women were every bit as intelligent as their minds.

What, then, is the nature of intelligence? What is the true measure of genius? The answer may be stated in a single word. That word is Desire.

20

ADAM KADMON

WHEN WE SPEAK OF ADAM KADMON, ALSO called Primordial Man, we are referring to the first stage of the first stage of emanation and hence the first level of limitation. From a cosmological standpoint it was the interval immediately following the Tsimtsum (known to science as the Big Bang) when Light and Vessel, energy and matter, were still intimately related by similarity of form. The universal condition extant at that time so closely resembled the state in the' Upper Light, where Light and Vessel were fused, that any distinction between them was almost imperceptible. Only later did the Light — from the standpoint of the Vessel — withdraw and vanish completely and the universe evolve to its present disunified form.

As with all phases of emanation, Adam Kadmon is subdivided into ten sefirothic components so as to clarify subsequent stages of development. The first of the first emanations, The Crown of Primordial Man, is described by the Ari, Rabbi Isaac Luria, as being, "the first circle — closely bound up with the Endless."

According to the Ari: "Afterwards, the line was drawn a bit more and then turned back so that a second circle was formed within the first. This is called, The Circle of Wisdom of Primordial Man. The Line continued and within the third circle emerged another which is referred to as, The Circle of Intelligence of Primordial Man, and so on until the tenth circle, the Circle of the Kingdom of Primordial Man was formed. Thus is explained the concept of the Ten Luminous Emanations or sefirot which emanated in the mysterious form of ten concentric circles."

Of course all of these primordial goings on have corollaries here on Malkhut in the present time. The immutable process of the emanations does not change to suit the fashion of the planetary seasons. We can see it in the stages of growth from a seed into a tree. The Crown of Adam Kadmon is the stage immediately after the seed has been planted but has not yet begun to grow. Only the slightest stirring of life has commenced, but it is as yet undetectable to the naked eye because the desire to receive has not yet become established.

Rather than being in a stage of unrevealment, as common logic would argue, the seed, from the kabbalistic perspective, having all of its inherent potentialities, is the most revealed

state — for that which is most revealed in the physical world is illusion and the greater the manifestation the greater the illusion. Only later, when the seed begins to grow, does the totality of the seed become obscured, and, as the old saying goes, "we can't see the forest for the trees."

The seed contains all of the future tree's stages, root, trunk, branch, leaf, and fruit. Each stage must be complete before the next one can begin, and yet, in a sense, each acts independently of the others. With each new embellishment the degree of separation is visually reinforced and the unity of the complete manifestation is further obscured. That is why, the kabbalist argues, it is essential for anyone seeking to understand the totality of nature to always return to the source.

MALKHUT

Malkhut, this lowest, most negative, of all worlds, is the only level capable of revealing Light of the highest order. Light, the absolute epitome of positiveness, illuminates man's Encircling Vessels to the exact degree to which the Desire to Receive is exercised. Light is revealed in the presence of Desire to Receive in direct proportion to the power of the intention, or force of will, by which it is drawn. The greater is the Desire to Receive, the greater is the potential to reveal. Having by far the most powerful will to receive, this world, Malkhut, is the level at which the greatest degree of Light is manifested.

We constantly remind the reader against literal interpretations of kabbalistic concepts. Here we should point out that while it is a normal reaction to attach disapproving connotations to terms such as "negative" and "lowest" which are used to describe Malkhut, the kabbalistic definitions of these words serve meanings not found in the dictionary. These terms refer to the degree to which Malkhut differs from the *Or En Sof* — Malkhut having the greatest dissimilarity is said to be lower and more negative than any of the other phases of existence.

Having little negativity (Desire to Receive) the first

three evolutionary phases, known variously as: Wisdom, Intelligence, and Beauty; Spirit, Soul, and Living; and also as Emanation, Creation, and Formation, manifest not *Or En Sof*, the Light of Creation. Here the cycle proceeds spontaneously with no effort on the part of these three phases. The first three grades of vegetal evolvement, namely, the roots, the trunk-branch complex, and the leaves, are stages in an automatic process, the purpose of which is to fulfill an inner need. In the plant kingdom it is the fruit which represents the fourth stage of evolvement. Only here is the purpose of the plant to procreate revealed in the seed contained within the fruit.

Just as a child must advance to a certain stage before realizing the nature of his or her existence, so must all things evolve involuntarily through the first three stages of growth, without awareness of their ultimate purpose. The Desire to Receive is revealed solely in the fourth phase. This fourth phase, Malkhut, is the stage at which the *Or En Sof*, having only a Desire to Impart, can find complete fulfillment.

When examined from this perspective, Malkhut, this most negative of worlds, begins to take on a new meaning. This fourth phase, Malkhut, and we who reside here are responsible for manifesting the Light of Creation. Does it not follow that rather than being the lowest stage of evolvement, Malkhut is really the highest phase? Kabbalistically speaking, the answer is both yes and no. That which is lowest always has potential to be highest and vice versa. Negative reveals positive, the vessel reveals Light. It is a kabbalistic principle that revealment comes about exclusively via the lowest, or fourth level, and what higher purpose can there be than revealing the Light of Creation?

The purpose of all worldly and otherworldly activity is to manifest Light, and this fourth phase, Malkhut, is the phase of revelation. Despite its drawbacks and the extreme negativity by which it is surrounded, Malkhut reveals Light. We dwellers on this lowest of all levels can take some small comfort in the knowledge that through our Desire to Receive we trigger this revealment.

The fourth, it may be said, is the only phase that has to work for a living. The other phases evolve automatically, without intervention on the part of the vessel, but the Curtain of the fourth phase must repel Light so as to bring Illumination not only to its own phase, the fourth, but to the higher phases by way of Returning Light. We of the fourth phase have to exert effort if we are to reveal Light. This condition was of our own making. We tried the easy way, but Bread of Shame caused us to relinquish our acceptance of the Creator's endless beneficence in favor of being able to exercise a degree of self-determination. Now, like it or not, we cannot return to the way we were, and we will not return, until the great life cycle is complete.

21

ONE EQUALS FOUR

A THOUGHT THAT SEEMS TO SPRING INTO our mind from out of nowhere is actually the end result, the Malkhut of a four phase process that has already happened in our unconscious mind. From another perspective, as strange as it may seem, that same thought is also the first stage, Keter, of a new four phase process that has the potential to become a physical reality. The Malkhut, or final revealment, is the fulfillment of a process that occurred in the stage above and it is also the Keter of the next stage below.

A simple example will serve to illuminate this concept. Being the least revealed aspect of a fruit, the seed is considered the fourth stage or Malkhut of that fruit, but if we remove the seed from the fruit, in effect revealing it, the same seed becomes the first phase or Keter of a potential new manifestation.

BEST LAID PLANS

A man may spend years organizing a new project or business venture, accounting for every detail and decimal point, mapping out every possible pitfall and contingency. He may have all of the necessary capital and qualifications, tools and expertise. He may have surrounded himself with top notch lawyers, planners, and financial advisors, and still his enterprise fails. Another man, meanwhile, possessing none of the former's qualifications, may jot on a napkin the blueprint for what will prove to be a multinational empire.

Examples abound of ventures that were planned to perfection but ended in failure. The Titanic and the Hindenberg stand out as conspicuous reminders of the best laid plans straying in most tragic ways. Both were marvels of planning, ingenuity, and technological achievement, yet both ultimately ended in disaster. Our own projects and investments may seem modest by comparison, but for us, of course, they are of utmost importance. We are all striving, with various degrees of intensity, to make our hopes, dreams, and ambitions into tangible assets.

Bread of Shame is the difference between dreams and realities. Consciously, or unconsciously, the one who succeeds must alleviate Bread of Shame which prevents the dream from linking with physicality. Possessions, whether they are physical or metaphysical, such as learning and knowledge, will not truly manifest without conscious effort, they must be earned. Those who do not take account of this fact may amass huge sums of money or other worldly possessions, but the Energy-Intelligence of that merchandise will not be owned by him, only the negative material trappings. The thief receives only the paper, but not the buying power of the money he steals. Never will he derive the same enjoyment from those commodities as the man who earned them.

Mesech, the curtain, must be lifted before any plan can manifest on this phase. The Curtain is the built-in safeguard without which the world would disappear. Were it not for the Curtain there would be no need for a physical existence. We would revert back to the undifferentiated state of perpetual giving on the part of the Emanator and taking on the part of the emanated in which we existed before the Tsimtsum. Mesech, the Curtain, and Tsimtsum, restriction, are the reasons why some ideas come to fruition, while others do not. It is essential for anyone who is intent on creating physical reality from the stuff of dreams to come to terms with the negativity that prevents the connection of his dream with the nature of his intentions.

The difference between a dream and actuality is the Curtain which does not permit the energy-intelligence of the Light to enter this phase unobstructed. The Curtain keeps us honest. It reminds us of our limitations. It is the force that prevents us from enjoying ill-gotten gains, the obstacle that stands between the planner and his plan, the dreamer and his dream. By removing the Curtain one allows the connection between his dream and the reality to be made. This is done by converting the Desire to Receive into a Desire to Receive for the Sake of Sharing. Only a clear conscience can lift the Curtain and thereby absolve us of Bread of Shame.

THE CLOSED CIRCUIT

That Desire is the root of all corruption is a kabbalistic principle, a keystone on which the foundation of Kabbalah was

constructed. Yet Desire, in and of itself, is not a sinful malediction. True, it is the root of all corruption, but it is also the source of all correction. No change, no friction, no correction of any kind, could take place without the Desire to Receive. The Light is still; the *Or En Sof* is Infinite and perfectly constant. Desire creates movement.

The Earth has a tremendous Desire to Receive (Gravity) which it exerts in an endless effort to draw to itself anything and everything within a wide radius of its field of influence — yet no one would accuse the Earth of avarice. This is because the Earth's Desire to Receive exists within a circular context. The Earth and all of her creatures — with the single exception of man — have an inborn restricting mechanism which seeks to balance cause with effect and compels them to take only according to specific needs and to give equal measure in return. Having no built-in restrictive mechanism, man falls easy prey to a debilitating malady peculiar only to his species: The Desire to Receive for Himself Alone, which might be loosely defined as Greed.

Laws are ways by which we seek to remedy this situation, but laws, no matter how strictly enforced, do not prevent crime. Advocates of capital punishment and stringent judicial penalties may argue that crime rates are statistically lower in those jurisdictions where so-called Law and Order policies are in effect, but that argument holds little water in view of the fact that thievery still exists in those countries where the penalty is the amputation of a hand, and murder is still committed in those places where the penalty is death.

Nor are morals and ethics — no matter how noble their intentions — any better at curbing the greedy appetites of man. Even the efficacy of the Ten Commandments must be questioned with respect to their attributable results, if any, on the actions of the human race. Man still lies, he cheats, he steals, he kills — in the three millennia that the Ten Commandments have been with us, his greed has not abated one iota, if anything it has increased. There seems to be no upper limit to man's inhumanity to man.

Yet all men are not imprisoned by avarice. A few are free of compulsions; a few can do without habitual crutches; a few are not self-absorbed to the point of self-destructiveness; a few are not so wrapped up in negativity as to be suffocating; a few are blessed with a clear conscience: a blessed few.

Why are some of us serving life sentences in a kind of negative purgatory, while others seem to roam free?

The simple answer is that some people live within a circular context — meaning that they have managed to transform the Desire to Receive for themselves into a Desire to Receive for the Sake of Imparting — while some have not. Some are able to combine their balanced best interests with the balanced best interests of others — some are not. This fourth phase, Malkhut, is steeped in negativity and we are all subject to its influence. We cannot escape it, but we can, by our positive thoughts and actions, turn it to our best advantage.

CRAVINGS

Desire stems from an inner longing which has already experienced its ultimate fulfillment. As we learned earlier, "It is impossible for any Desire to be stirred up in Existence unless at a previous time a fulfillment was revealed sufficient to that Desire." Now the Ari teaches us that, "Desire in the Upper Worlds becomes potential and a necessity in the Lower Worlds."

Any physical effect is initiated by a cause on the metaphysical plane. As the *En Sof* was the cause of everything, it follows that It also encompassed every desire and every fulfillment that was, is, or ever will be. Every desire one may have is already fulfilled in a potential state, every sculpture has been sculpted, every building built, every wish has already been potentially granted. Fulfillment precedes desire. The effect is contained within the cause.

Having known fulfillment is it any wonder that we can have no rest, no sense of completion, until our inner encircling vessels have been restored to their former splendor?

We could not possibly long for anything of which we have no conception. A native of the rain forest is no more likely to suddenly develop an urgent craving for chocolate truffles than a westerner is likely to be seized by a desire for the live grubs which the native treasures as a delicacy. Craving do not spring up of their own volition, the taste must have been tasted before.

The very stuff of which the human body is composed — the atoms in our blood, the electrons that spur the impulses in our brains, the chemicals that make up our tissue and our bones — have roots in the *En Sof* before the Thought of Creation. All of the various natural forces and energy-intelligences, all physical matter, anti-matter, and subatomic tendencies have existed since before the dawn of time.

We have all known the Endless One. We have experienced unity with the Force of Creation. We have tasted of the sweet fruit of perfection. Why do we not remember? The answer is we do. Only our minds have forgotten. The rest of us remembers, our blood, our genes, our bones. The memory lingers in our soul. It is impressed into our circular vessels. The Force is a part of us, but the Curtain and the Tsimtsum prevent us from remembering. It must be so. Otherwise, we would have no opportunity for correction, no way of absolving Bread of Shame.

22

PARTZUF

THE EMANATION OF A COMPLETE STRUCTURE is called *partzuf*, meaning face or countenance. Each *partzuf* embodies all five sefirot or levels of emanation: Keter (Crown), Hochmah (Wisdom), Binah (Intelligence), Tiferet (Beauty), and Malkhut (Kingdom). The fourth Sefira, Tiferet, includes the Sefirot: Hesed (Mercy), Gevurah (Judgment), Tiferet (Beauty), Netzah (Victory), Hod (Majesty), and Yesod (Foundation). It should be noted that a *partzuf*, as does every manifestation, physical and metaphysical, is made up of a full complement of ten sefirot, and that each *partzuf* is caused by, yet distinct from, the structure that emerged one stage before.

The root of a plant must take hold before the trunk can manifest, the trunk before the branches, the branches before the leaves. All things, animal, vegetable, and mineral, evolve through this same, never-varying process of four emanations. Each of the

four emanations is a *partzuf* , a complete structure, distinct from
the stages that precede it and follow it, yet almost identical and
thereby related by way of Similarity of Form. Just as each of the
four seasons plays a distinct role in the completion of a solar cycle,
so too must each person proceed through four distinct, yet inter-
connected, evolutionary seasons so as to complete the cycle of his
or her existence.

Nothing can come fully into the Light without the emanation of four distinct stages. Each *partzuf* must be complete before
the next one can emerge into being. Of all the creatures on this
planet only we have the ability to bring this process to a conscious
level and to adapt it to serve as a means for cosmic awareness and
personal awakening.

LASTING IMPRESSIONS

Before the great restriction known to kabbalists as the
Tsimtsum, we the emanated asked for and received the eternal and
inalienable aspect of free will which allows us to reveal the Light
or not reveal It as we so choose. The Light that once filled our
inner Encircling Vessels restricted and withdrew, but certain
"impressions" or "residues" remained in them. These echoes of our
former completeness allow us to find no rest, no fulfillment, until
the now seemingly vacant sefirot again sparkle with Infinite
Illumination.

Bread of Shame caused us to close our eyes to the Light of
Creation. The Tsimtsum made the Vessel blind to the Light. No
longer would the Vessel receive the Light's boundless beneficence.
From that instant onward it became the Vessel's task to reveal the

Light. Only a minute fraction of the former Illumination remained in the ten circular sefirot. These almost imperceivable reverberations stir a longing in the Vessels which prevent them from resting until they draw in all the Light that once filled them.

The Ari called this lingering Illumination "impressions" or "residues." More recently some kabbalists have adopted terms such as, "vibrations," "echoes," and "reverberations" in reference to the connotation of the power inherent in the sefirot as being "Music of the Spheres." All of these terms indicate that the circular vessels are empty of revelation, but the "impression" remains, and, as always, the reader is advised to adopt the words that create the strongest internal connections.

The impressions act as a constant unconscious reminder that we once were an undifferentiated aspect of the Infinite Light of Creation. While we may not know it these faint reverberations of our former unity with the *Or En Sof* launch our every move and maneuver, decision and desire.

In actuality, all of our desires are aspects of only one desire. We have but one aspiration and that is to restore to our inner Encircling Vessels the full measure of Infinite Illumination with which they once were blessed. The circular sefirot and the impressions etched into them are the driving force behind our very existence.

Only by reestablishing communication with the Light through the limited creative process of the Line can our singular fulfillment again be revealed — the same aspect of Illumination that satiated all Desire before Bread of Shame was alleviated through the withdrawal and Restriction. Through the conscious application of restriction (the Line) we reconnect our cables with the Light of Creation. This is the method by which the kabbalist restores Light to the inner Encircling Vessels and sheds Illumination on all that enters within his or her circle of influence.

23

THE FIRST THREE

KABBALAH RECOGNIZES FOUR DISTINCT, through interrelated, phases of emanation. The evolution of any physical entity or non-physical emanation is a four phase process. There is a further division of each phase into ten subdivisions (named after the ten sefirot) and each of those stages is again divided by ten, and so on into Infinity. Every manifestation must proceed through the same four phase process to complete the cycle of its existence.

Any manifestation, whether physical or metaphysical, that does not advance according to the laws of cause and effect through all four stages and all the myriad sub-stages cannot possibly reach completion. The interruption of the four phases accounts for seeds that do not come to fruition, plans that go astray, thoughts that get sidetracked, and enterprises that fail to "get off the ground."

The stage on which we are now focusing, the first of the first, is actually three phases: Keter (Crown), Hochmah (Wisdom), and Binah (Understanding). These three energy-intelligences together are known as The Head, and also as The First Three. The First Three precede both physical and metaphysical emanation by connecting with the potential of each new phase. The reason they are grouped together is that they operate beyond the realm of everyday consciousness and precede the observable phases of physical manifestation. Having great affinity with the Light and little similarity with the world of restriction, The First Three exist in an almost totally purified state, remaining, like the inner operation of a seed, invisible to the naked eye and beyond the realm of normal waking consciousness.

For purposes of clarification, The First Three can be likened to the point of a pencil. Before a person picks up a pencil The First Three must have already made a connection on a metaphysical (thought) level with the end result of whatever it is that the person hopes to manifest. A subconscious activity has taken place in which the completed drawing or writing has already in some sense been completed in the mind. This non-observable action is called The First Three. The moment the tip of the pencil touches the paper a new phase begins, that of the physical process. Again The First Three are active, making the potential connections, but this time on the fourth (physical) level of emanation. When the tip of the pencil begins to move the world of restriction becomes manifest, beginning the next phase of the ten stage process.

The First Three, Keter, Hochmah, ad Binah, play a vital behind-the-scenes role in every thought and physical manifestation. Though active only in the potential state they must still be considered a part of every creative process. They are active, connecting potentialities. The beauty of potential is that it has affinity with potential everywhere. Potential is not a part of the world of Restriction, but rather an attribute of the Endless. All of us are blessed with an almost infinite abundance of potential which can connect with potential in any dimension. This act of connecting potentialities is the first step in any thought, growth, or physical manifestation.

The Crown of Adam Kadmon

Adam Kadmon is the first frame of reference after the Tsimtsum. When we speak of the Crown (Keter) of Adam Kadmon we are referring to the root of the root, the seed of the seed, the first world, the first level of fulfillment in the Circular Vessels. This is an unseen world, closely aligned with the Infinite, the operation of which takes place beyond the realm of the common senses. Why then should we bother to study it?

Physicists are the first to inform us that we see but a fraction of what goes on around us. Even with the most powerful telescopes we can see but a tiny portion of the universe, and, conversely, even the strongest electron microscopes reveal only an infinitesimal fraction of the entire spectrum of atomic activity and absolutely nothing of the subatomic realm. An apple would have to be expanded to the size of the earth to see one of its atoms with the naked eye, and beneath that atomic world is another world, the ratio of which is even greater than that of the atom with the physical world. So when kabbalists tell us that the vast majority of what goes on in this universe is beyond the realm of finite understanding they know well of what they speak.

Still that does not answer the question of why it is necessary or even prudent to consider that which we can never see.

Simple observation should tell us that the final manifestation of any event has nothing to do with the truth. History is full
of examples of governmental machinations that "pull the wool"
over the eyes of the populace. A recent example of diversionary
tactics was the ruse concerning terrorism by which a frightened
populace stays home, adding huge sums to the domestic treasury,
while at the same time diverting the public's attention from
domestic issues such as poverty and unemployment, when in fact
four times more Americans die annually of being struck by light-
ening than are killed by terrorists.

This isolated incident is not cited here to denigrate politicians, for they are by no means the only parties guilty of hiding
the truth in order to achieve some self-serving end. Advertisers gloss
over the bad features of the often shoddy merchandise they are ped-
dling. Lawyers pile lie upon lie so that the "truth will prevail."
Doctors prescribe drugs that hide the symptoms without effecting a
cure. In fact, in this the observable world, this tiny fraction of the
spectrum of existence, one would be hard pressed to find anything
with even the faintest resemblance to the truth. Indeed, the kabbalist will tell you that looking for truth in this the world of illusion is
like trying to find a subatomic particle in a haystack.

The kabbalist seeks to understand the source of all things.
To accept the observable world as the totality of existence is to
cheat oneself out of the vast majority of life's possibilities. The
term used earlier "pull the wool over the eyes" as well as other
expressions from the common vernacular such as "snow job" and

"smoke screen" imply a covering over of the truth. To the kabbalist's way of thinking this entire phase of existence is covered over by negativity (klippot) and is hence deemed illusionary.

The Ari gave us a system by which to penetrate the crust of illusion that surrounds this world and find the Infinite reality within. No longer need we accept at face value the lies that pose as truth. Instead of being enslaved by deception we can become, to some degree, the masters of our fates. Through the Lurianic system we can plant the seeds of our own creation in the vast fields of our potential that now lie fallow. By taking part in the process of our own spiritual evolution, we learn to resist that which is illusion in favor of that which is at the source of existence, the real, the metaphysical truth.

AFFINITY

Only the first three sefirot Keter, Hochmah, and Binah, of the sefirot of straightness (Line), can meld and be encircled by the ten sefirot of Keter of the circular vessels (Circle). The First Three, you will remember, exist in a non-observable state of potential. Potential has affinity with potential. Like attracts like. Hence, the affinities in The First Three of the Line can connect with the affinities of ten Circular vessels. This blending of similarities is the first of many stages in which the finite and the infinite unite for the sake of mutual revealment.

The frame of reference is Adam Kadmon which has ten sefirot, but more specifically we are dealing with only The First Three (sefirot), Keter, Hochmah, Binah, of the ten sefirot of Adam Kadmon. Adam Kadmon represents the highest possible state of finite existence, the totality of all that was created. If Adam Kadmon were any closer to Infinite perfection He and we would revert back to the original condition in which it is said that, "He and his Name were One." It is for this reason that Adam Kadmon, who should not be confused with Adam HaRishon, the mythic man of the garden, is considered within a Circular (Infinite) context.

As Kabbalah is a multi-layered study, the reader should be aware that while we are discussing the emergence of the world of creation we are also speaking of the first emergence of self-aware-ness. Through our conscious re-enactment of the Tsimtsum, known as the Line, we send out tenuous, potential "strands" of affinity to The First Three of our own unique, unrevealed perfection, the inner Encircling sefirot. Only when the Keter, Hochmah, Binah of the Line, is encircled by the ten sefirot of our Circles, can the process begin by which the unrevealed Light within our inner Encircling (Infinite) vessels can again be illuminated.

Only the first three sefirot of the ten sefirot of the Crown (Keter) of the Line are embraced by all ten sefirot of the Circles. The first three sefirot of the Line have complete affinity with all of the ten Encircling sefirot, whereas the seven lower sefirot of straightness (the Line) have no affinity with the ten sefirot of Keter of the Encircling vessels. The result is that the Encircling Vessels, whose Light is unrevealed, can never be fully illuminated through the limited process of the Line. The simple explanation for this is that the straight vessels are a product of finitude while the circular vessels are a part of the Infinite. Always there must be a dissimilarity of phase between the two. Otherwise we return back to the condition before Tsimtsum in which we the emanated had no opportunity for correction.

ON A SCALE OF ONE TO TEN

The moment a baby is born the doctor or midwife in attendance counts the toes and fingers. If the total in each case is ten the child is declared "perfect." Mathematics, our most perfect invention (in the sense of being absolute), is based on ten. A physically attractive person is apt to be declared a "Ten" by members of the opposite sex. From hit parades to movie and restaurant reviews, it seems that almost everything in this physical realm of existence, is measured on a scale of one to ten. Ten is also the number of totality in the dominions of the metaphysical.

Every thought, every manifestation, physical or metaphysical, must advance through four phases, each with ten stages, the Ten Sefirot or Luminous Emanations. This aspect of ten exists whether we are considering empty circular vessels or the ten sefirot of straightness. Earth (solids), sea (liquids), sky (gasses), it matters not of what we speak, the ten attributes, or sefirot, each of which is comprised of infinite permutations of ten within ten within ten, are present in every star and planet, every speck of cosmic dust in the universe.

The root must take hold before the trunk can manifest, the trunk before the branches, and so on. The root is a product of a ten stage process, as is the trunk, the branches, the leaves, and the fruit. Each stage is a necessary component in the completed manifestation. In the same manner as a person learns through experience and, it is hoped, from mistakes, so does each thought, word, deed, and evolving entity, acquire a certain residual knowledge of the essence of each sefira. Those characteristics are carried forward until a full aggregate of ten qualities has been accumulated. Thus do we acquire the requisite attributes for a completed physical or metaphysical existence.

Each sefira has what might be described as an unique "atmosphere" which distinguishes it from the other nine sefirot. Keter, the first stage, is deemed the highest, purest phase by virtue of being closest to the source, the *Or En Sof*. Like the other sefirot and phases of emanation, Keter must also pass though ten stages, but being closely aligned with the Infinite, its inner workings occur completely beyond the range of the senses.

Keter, having, having almost no desire to receive, has virtually nothing in common with the seven lower sefirot, but a great deal of affinity with Hochmah and Binah, whose workings also transcend the realm of finite understanding. And it is for this reason, as we learned earlier, that Keter, Hochmah, and Binah, are considered as a single stage known as the Head, or The First Three. From Keter, through Hochmah and Binah, Hesed and Gevurah, and so on, the density of the "atmosphere," or "negativity," or "thickness," or dissimilarity with the Endless, increases until the evolving thought or entity finally arrives at the tenth and last sefira, which has the least affinity with the Endless, this fourth World of Resistance, Malkhut.

The process of ten within ten repeats four.times, once for each of the four phases of emanation, before the entity or manifestation reaches completion. In other words, Wisdom, the first phase of emanation, advances through the same ten stage process of Keter, Hochmah, Binah, Hesed, Gevurah, Tiferet, Hod, Netzah, Yesod, and Malkhut, before the next phase of emanation, known as Intelligence, can begin. After Intelligence, the second phase of emanation, has completed its ten stage cycle, the third phase of emanation known as Beauty advances through its ten stage cycle, and finally the fourth and last phase of emanation, Kingdom, evolves through ten stages at the end of which the preceding stages of evolution are at last revealed on the physical level.

24

DENSITY

WHEN THE ARI TAUGHT US THAT ALL VESSELS and material of creation are drawn from the World of Restriction he was not alluding to a situation in which the vessels and material of which he was speaking were actually drawn or moved through space-time. Rather, in the kabbalistic lexicon, the word drawn refers to that which becomes "thickened" or "impure" by virtue of being farther from the *Or En Sof*.

Just as the air becomes thinner as we rise through the strata of Earth's atmosphere, so too may it be said that the "atmosphere" of the metaphysical levels becomes less dense, and is hence deemed purer and higher as we withdraw from The World of Restriction. That which is farther from the Light, is defined as being thicker and less pure than that which is closer to the Endless. The greater is its dissimilarity of form with the Endless, the greater is the degree of impurity, and this world, Malkhut, the

World of Restriction, being possessed of a tremendous Desire to Receive is, in the kabbalistic frame of reference, negative or impure to an extreme degree.

A person's purity, or lack of it, is measured according to the degree of affinity he or she has with the Light. Those manifesting great Desire to Receive for Oneself Alone are considered by Kabbalah to have little affinity with the Endless and are hence deemed lower and less pure than those who convert the Desire to Receive into Desire for the Sake of Imparting.

LESS IS MORE

If there is one word that could define advanced technology, the concept of reductionism would say it all. The race for small components in hi-tech is in full swing. The smaller the product, the chances for success is so much greater. Smaller microchips that can transfer larger amounts of information is a primary objective for today's scientist.

What we are witnessing today is the realization that the landscape of computers has been radically transformed by the loss of corporeal matter. Microchips become smaller and smaller and density greater. The new work has focused not on the power of mathematical computational but on its size.

In a mere 25 years computers have become so fast at processing information — a third of a billion times faster than they could in the early 1960s — that their powers numb the comprehension.

They have also changed our lives-by permitting instantaneous worldwide tele-communications, miniaturization of integrated circuits permitting sophisticated home computers, to name a few examples.

Common sense tells us that a communications cable's capacity should shrink with its diameter. In the case of fiberoptics, common sense is wrong. Today's hair-thin glass fibers can carry more information farther than metal cables thicker than a man's arm.

Generally speaking, an elaborate excuse for failing to live up to some expectation is less believable than a short, concise explanation. Speeches long on words, but short on substance, are less likely to sway the listener than those that stick to the issues. Complex international espionage thrillers brimming with tricky sub-plots, extraneous characters, globe-hopping, and needless elaborations may engage the reader's interest and even keep him turning pages furiously, but in the end the reader is often left with the feeling that he has somehow been "had." More effective is a story told in a straight forward manner with sympathetic characters and an identifiable theme.

Less is more.

A simple song is likely to be more accessible to the average listener than a complex one. A lawyer with a strong case will present the simple facts, while the lawyer with the weaker case uses the "buckshot approach" which attempts to impress the jury with the sheer bulk of inconsequential evidence. The truth needs no embellishment. Scientists search for a simple solution by which to explain the workings of nature. Artists in the movement known as "minimalism" affirm the power of visual images which have been "stripped to the bone."

Less is more.

This concept takes some getting used to. Today, in modern industrialized societies, bigness has become synonymous with quality. "The bigger the better" is the catch phrase of the day. Young people, both male and female, are "bulking up" as never before. Today we adulate that which is "larger than life." Sports stars with nicknames such as "The Refrigerator" decorate our TV screens. Large, poorly designed, shoddily constructed, gas-guzzling cars are making a comeback. People flock by the millions to have their eardrums split by enormous trucks with ten-foot-high tires and thousand horse-power engines that crush cars while spewing mud and pollution.

Today's modern society judges people by the bulk of their possessions, envying those with the most and pitying those with the least. Yet history is filled with stories of men like Howard Hughes and women like Hettie Green (who lived like a pauper while possessing millions) who were imprisoned by their riches. A fast food factory may serve more food than any other distributor in the world and yet no one who has tasted real food would say that the quality of fast junk food is in any way the equal of good home cooking. Skyscrapers, though they may be the tallest buildings in the world, and even beautiful in their own right, cannot compare in quality with the Taj Mahal or other handmade structures which are minuscule by comparison.

Less is more.

This metaphysical paradox goes against the grain of contemporary popular culture. Undoubtedly it will be some time before it is understood much less accepted by fans of monster trucks and professional wrestling, much less embrace, the kabbalistic notion that physicality is unreality — the denser the physical matter the greater the illusion.

Yet, were they to compare the energy produced by dynamite with that produced by the splitting of an atom — the lesser corporeal matter producing infinitely more energy — it is possible that they might begin to break through the conceptual barrier that prevents such a transformation from being feasible. And were they to consider the limited sending capacity of copper wire with the far superior ability of much less fiber optical material, they might acquire still more understanding of this principle. And were they to compare the taste of a fruit picked at the peak of season with a much larger fruit that was left too long on the vine, they might suddenly find themselves actually agreeing with the idea that less really is more. True this possibility is remote in the extreme, but then again anything is possible.

BREAKING THROUGH

It is said that when Rabbi Isaac Luria studied the Zohar the flame of his desire burned so intensely that perspiration would quite literally pour off him. Through his studies he absorbed, converted, and transformed negativity (klippot) and thus became a channel for the *Or En Sof*. That his efforts were rewarded is evidenced by the fact that Lurianic Kabbalah has survived intact for over five centuries.

Rabbi Ashlag, the twentieth century kabbalist, philosopher, and translator of the classic sixteen volume work based on the Ari's teachings, Ten Luminous Emanations, contended that breaking through to self awareness required only one prerequisite — a quality for which Rabbi Luria was obviously not lacking — that attribute is desire.

THE HEAD-BODY DICHOTOMY

The first three sefirot, Keter, Hochmah, and Binah are called, The Head. It stands to reason, then, that the lower seven, Hesed (Mercy), Gevurah (Judgment), Tiferet (Beauty), Hod (Glory), Netzah (Victory), Yesod (Foundation), and Malkhut (Kingdom), should be called, The Body. And so they are.

The Body, like us, is a part of the World of Restriction. The human body is a shaft of material substance, a Line, that stands up from the earth. From birth to death it struggles against gravity. All its life it must exert an outward force of 14.7 pounds of pressure per square inch to combat the effects of air pressure. The Body has a beginning, a middle, and an end. The Body dies.

The Head operates outside the scope of rational comprehension, beyond logic, beyond the senses. The Head is Endless, it is part of the Infinite. And being of a Circular or Infinite nature, it is not affected in the least by restriction and negative constraints. The Head can merge with anyone or anything. It never dies, but continues on in Circles of Return.

Being finite, then, it follows that the only information we finite beings can possibly glean concerning the Infinite First

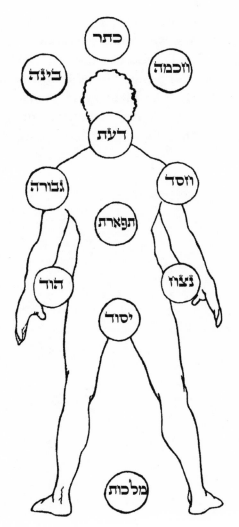

Three, must be through observing the Body, the lower seven. Also, as Kabbalah is an edifice of many stories, it must be true that this concept of three and seven can be viewed from a personal perspective — meaning the body, the human body, being of a finite nature, can have no affinity with the head, the human head.

Yet previous chapters assured us that every sefira is comprised of all ten attributes and therefore even the sefirot that make up our bodies must also include the Infinite Head or First Three, which would mean that the First Three in our heads and in our bodies do have affinity with the Light. How, then, can it be that our bodies have no affinity with something that is an integral part of them?

The answer is that The Head and the Body are separated by a Curtain which prevents the two from communicating, but only in the Body or lower seven The Curtain does not hinder the operation of the Head, the reason being that the Infinite is never affected by that which is finite. The Light never changes. The Light eclipses darkness whenever the two come into contact — the Infinite holding that which is finite in a state of suspended animation.

25

THE PARADOX

MANY, IF NOT ALL, HUNTER-GATHERER societies believed in a mythical trickster deity. The Indians of the Northwest coast had the Raven. In the southwest and other places it was Coyote. Thor, the Morse god was a trickster. Brer Rabbit, Reynard the Fox, and the Joker in the deck of playing cards are all pale continuations on this ancient, venerable theme. The hunter-gatherers recognized the paradox and found pleasure in it. They could not solve the riddle or life — so they celebrated it!

When the hunter-gatherers settled down to more sedentary lives of farming and raising livestock everything changed. No longer could people find humor in the tricksters of old. The coyote, instead of being a clever, laughable little fellow became a hated, hunted animal who stole chickens and killed sheep. The fox, in merry old England, became the subject of cruel hunts on horseback ~y which 1 civilized" man could attempt to express his superiority over the trickster, the mystery, the uncertainty of life.

Slowly, the paradox which was the trickster deity was covered over with new theories, validations, and beliefs. Religions sought to protect us from the paradox. Philosophies sought to white-wash it. And over the years the mystical relationship that early man enjoyed with life's uncertainty was eroded, replaced by mountains of impossible explanations, ridiculous precepts, rules, regulations and superstitious beliefs. At last, Science, with its false promise that all things would one day be explained, sounded the death knell for the trickster.

And a sad day it was for us all.

Of course the trickster never died, the paradox remains as unexplainable, as irreconcilable as it ever was. Still religions try to protect us from it, but it pops up between the words of even the most charismatic evangelist. New scientific theories still seek to explain it, but they never will. Television attempts to homogenize it, but the moment we press the off button the paradox returns.

The paradox is dead. Long live the paradox!

The only light we see is reflected light. Light is darkness until it is revealed through the process of Binding by Striking. The Light is there, but because of Tsimtsum and the Curtain our eyes are blind to its Infinite brilliance. Were it not for Binding by Striking no light would be visible to us. The paradox is that through restriction we create affinity with the ultimate in non-restriction, the Light of the Endless. And the greater the capacity for resistance the greater is the revelation of the Light.

In this the World of Restriction which is also the world of revelation, it is a physical and a metaphysical truth that the greater the degree of resistance, the brighter will be the revelation of Light. Strike one rock against another and a spark will be produced, strike it again, this time with more force, and the spark will be larger. When we focus the light of the sun through a magnifying glass (restriction) onto a sheet of paper, eventually it bursts into names. The smaller is the point of focus (the greater the restriction) the more forceful will be the revealment or release when the paper begins to burn. The larger is the capacity for resistance of the filament of a light bulb the more light will that bulb manifest. In every instance light is the product of resistance, and the greater the restriction the greater is the revealment of Light.

The harder one concentrates on something (restriction on one train of thought) the more notable will be the breakthrough in terms of one's thinking. Take as another example the production of sound. The harder a string is struck with a plectrum, the louder will be the note. The greater is the force of compression on a membrane, the more forceful will be the percussive effect. No sound can manifest, no light, no thought, nothing at all in this World of Restriction, without resistance, and the greater the resistance the greater is the manifestation.

Art, literature, music, philosophy, no matter what the field of endeavor, the larger is the capacity for restriction, the more magnanimous will be the outpouring of Light. The paradox arises even when we are doing the dishes or mowing the lawn. Sometimes, when we are bored with our work, or have other "more important" things to do, time drags by and our energy becomes so drained that it is almost impossible, it seems, to go on.

Yet the moment we decide to apply ourselves to the same task something happens. By concentrating, focusing, restricting our focus we release new energy, the job goes faster, and when it is accomplished we have energy enough to take on the world.

By resisting we create affinity with the original restriction and the first act of Creation, Tsimtsum. When we restrict our Desire to Receive for Ourselves Alone we create a Circular affinity with the Light. This is how our original desire which was a negative characteristic of the Line is converted into Desire for the Sake of Sharing. Through resistance we manifest that which is Endless, peaceful, and perfectly still. By saying no we arrive at yes. This is the paradox. And may it always remain a mystery.

INFERIORITY

The Curtain, as mentioned earlier, is inoperative in the First Three of the Encircling Sefirot. It is, however, fully activated in all ten Sefirot of the lower seven. Imagine a family of ten sitting in a circle on a sunny day when a black curtain descends from the sky, dividing the circle into groups of three and seven. The group of three is on the sunny side of the curtain while the other seven are shaded by the curtain. The family is still in a circle, but now, from the perspective of an observer on the shaded side, it appears as if there are only seven people, and from the point of view of the sunny side it appears as if there are only three.

The group of three is still bathed in sunlight. For them the light is of identical intensity to what it was before. From the perspective of the group of seven, however, who have come under the influence of the curtain, it appears as if the light has dimmed. Imagine now that the curtain is soundproof, creating a situation in which the two groups cannot communicate in any way. The two groups of three and seven cannot perceive with their common senses the people on opposite sides of the curtain, but they know full well that nothing has changed. Each experiences a sense of loss at having their circle divided and the only way to alleviate that feeling is by lifting the curtain thereby restoring the family to its original circular condition — which is exactly what they would set out to do.

What the Ari meant when he taught us that the seven sefirot that follow the Curtain are inferior to the first three, then, was not that there was any internal difference between them. The inferiority of which he was speaking is in no way connected with sefirot themselves — just as the seven people behind the curtain are not inferior to the other three, nor has anything of their essential nature been changed or lessened. The only difference between them is the result of the negative (darkening) power of the Curtain.

Whether we are speaking of sunlight or the metaphysical Light of Creation, the intensity of Light never changes. In the kabbalistic frame of reference the light on the sunny side of the curtain is identical to the light on the shaded side. The Light is everywhere. It glows with equal intensity in the center of the earth as it does in the center of the sun. The eternal Light of Creation can never be diminished — any more than painting a light bulb black can in any way lessen the energy produced by the bulb. The difference arises only as a result of the illusion presented by the Curtain from the perspective of all that comes under its negative influence.

The purpose of Kabbalah is to remove that illusion.

26

BEYOND THE COMMON SENSES

WE STAKE CAREERS ON "COMMON SENSE" decisions. Cars and houses are purchased. Investments are made. Schools and colleges are chosen. Diets are planned. Debts are paid. Laws are passed and broken. Contracts are signed. Work is undertaken. Vacations are arranged. Moves are made. Contacts are developed. The ties of friendship and even marriage are initiated and maintained.

Common sense rules our very lives.

Common sense — what is it? That question will elicit as many different responses as there are people of who it is asked. Common sense is one of these relative expressions that everyone takes for granted as having a common connotation, but which really means different things to different people. For in fact what may seem perfectly sensible to one person may seem illogical or even totally nonsensical to another.

All of us can cite examples in our lives when some action we took which seemed sensible in the beginning led in the end to a less than positive result. Often we go against the grain of our natural inclinations to do what common sense dictates, only to discover that our natural instincts were right. Common sense, it seems, has an almost hypnotic quality. It lulls us into following it down the proverbial garden path and just when we are smelling the flowers of what we thought were our correct decisions we fall into a hole at the bottom of which is a metaphorical alligator or a sharp stick. Common sense is a trap into which many of us fall.

Kabbalah teaches us ways to get out of that trap. Just as the principles of Kabbalah cannot be perceived by the five common senses, nor can logic, reason, and common sense lead us to find the source of the river of our being. The Light cannot be learned, it must be experienced. Metaphysical connections cannot be made by means of the intellect — the tentacles of cosmic awareness proceed from the heart. That is not to imply that common sense and logic do not have their place, for they do. It is only when trial and error methods have failed that one begins — some might say through common sense — to understand that in spiritual matters the five common senses are not enough.

The purpose of Kabbalah is to remove the chains of logic and reason so that we may be released from the cage of our five common senses, for it is only by transcending the limits of these self-made linear boundaries that a direct link with the cosmic forces can be made. Only then can the real inner journey begin.

INSANITY

Pity the madman. He lives in a world of fantasy and make believe. He knows nothing of the world of "what is." The poor fellow, it is said, has no conception of reality. Yet, perhaps in his imagination he is the ruler of a great nation; perhaps in his delusions he lives in a castle where servants attend his every need; perhaps, in his world of perpetual fantasy, he winters in Switzerland and spends sunsoaked summers languishing on the sandy beaches of St. Tropez.

For this he should be pitied?

Now pause to examine a man who by contemporary social standards, is judged sane. Anything but happy, our so-called sane man fights a constant, losing battle with the imagined forces that seek to destroy him. Life is an endless struggle for dominance over the material plane. A workaholic with an ulcer, he keeps twice weekly appointments with a psychiatrist who does his best to assure him that it is not really a dog eat dog world, but as far as our sane man is concerned life boils down to one decision: Kill or be killed, eat or be eaten. For him, "it's a jungle out there." He claims to be, "swimming in shark-infested waters." And though his psychiatrist may not know it, the world imagined by our friend, the sane man, is truly his reality. By choosing to live by the laws of the jungle he has become a creature of the jungle. By adopting a shark's mentality he has become a shark. For him it is a dog eat dog world of eat or be eaten, and little by little the dogs of his own imagination are chewing him down to the bone.

Meanwhile, our madman, who "in reality" lives in a mental institution, falls asleep the moment his head touches the pillow and he dreams peaceful, kingly dreams. When morning comes the orderly who wakens him is not a hospital worker. In his demented state of mind, the entire staff of the hospital exists for the sole purpose of giving him pleasure. The breakfast served to him by his personal entourage of servants and handmaidens, while probably quite bland and tasteless by ordinary worldly standards, is, for him, a smorgasbord of royal delicacies. And after breakfast, depending on the season, he is off once again to the sunny slopes of Switzerland, or roaming the sandy shores of St. Tropez.

Back to our friend the sane man. At night he arrives home, one of the world weary walking wounded, defeated by another day. Two small strangers, his children, barely manage mumbled greetings while staring blankly at the TV screen. A hastily scrawled note from his wife reminds him that the TV Dinners are still kept in the freezer. He has a drink while his supper is cooking and daydreams about the vacation he needs so desperately, the vacation for which he has been saving all year. After supper he has two more drinks to calm him down. Later he goes to bed, but so filled is he with anxiety, that he cannot sleep. He takes some pills, but even the strongest prescription medications do little to alleviate the worries that haunt him night and day. From the drawer of the nightstand beside his bed he removes the itinerary for his vacation. For an hour he stares at the glossy, four-color pictures of the sun-drenched sands of St. Tropez, where, in only a matter of months, he will at last escape the worries of his stress-filled life — if he lives that long.

The madman, in the meantime, has decided to become a movie star and in his imagination he has landed the leading role in the latest Woody Allen movie. Modesty prevents him from talking much about the recent Olympic gold medal he won for downhill ski racing. Nor does he boast about the time he addressed the United Nations. People would think he was crazy.

The long-awaited day of departure has at last arrived for our sane man and his family. This vacation is going to be the best one they have ever had, even if it bankrupts him. After a seven hour flight they deplane in Europe, exhausted. He and his wife are not speaking. The children are in foul moods. An hour long ride at high speed on rainsoaked cobblestones brings them to the expensive hotel at which they will be spending the next three weeks. A hurricane is blowing. The taxi lurches off with some of their baggage — the driver "forgot" to give him his change. Our sane man's mood becomes even darker when he and his family arrive at the suite, which instead of overlooking the Mediterranean, as expected, has a good view of the airport which is no more than a five minute walk away.

By coincidence our madman happens to be staying in the same hotel. Of course all this is happening only in his imagination, but not being there in person has its advantages. For instance, upon arrival in a limousine which was driven by his own personal chauffeur, our madman was spirited by attentive servants directly to the penthouse suite from which the view of the Mediterranean is beyond compare. The weather is perfect. And to top it off, all this extravagance is not costing him a penny because he owns the hotel and the mile-long stretch of sundrenched beach on which it stands.

By morning, the sane man's ulcer is acting up. His night

was a nightmare. A wild party in the suite above precluded any possibility of sleep until sometime after four a.m. and when at last it ended he and his family received a series of courtesy wake-up calls which they did not order. Still, he struggles out of bed, determined that this vacation will be the best he has ever had — even if it kills him.

And, sadly, it nearly does. The next three weeks are no better. Try as he might our sane man cannot escape the pressurized cabin of his mind. And when his vacation is over, when all is said and done, the sane man returns to the world of stress and strain, the dog eat dog world in which so many of us have chosen to live, the jungle where only the strongest survive, the shark-infested waters in which it is always a case of eat or be eaten — a world in which only a madman could be happy.

And what ever happened to our madman? The poor fellow is still a man to be pitied. He cannot seem to rid himself of the insane notion that he is a king. He continues to imagine himself skiing the Swiss Alps, starring in movies, winning gold medals, and occasionally addressing the General Assembly of the U.N.. His doctors hold little hope for him. The prognosis is bad. They say if something is not done soon, our poor madman is in imminent danger of being overcome by delusions of peace and happiness.

27

THE LINE OF MOST RESISTANCE

TEMPTATION COMES AT US IN A CONSTANT barrage. Advertising leaps out from billboards and television screens, tempting us to buy that which we do not need and cannot afford. Attractive models beckon from the glossy pages of books and magazines, enticing us to drink, smoke, gamble, consume drugs, and act licentiously. Some of us surrender rarely to those temptations, others regularly, some continually. Habitual surrenders, in contemporary Western cultures, are absolved of responsibility for their vices by use of a convenient, but erroneous, catch-all concept: "Addictive personality."

The idea of resistance takes some getting used to. Today, in a modern sophisticated society, "instant," "new" demands have become synonymous with quality. Have a headache? "Fast, fast relief" is the catch phrase of the day. Let's face it; who wants a lingering, painful headache.

However successful the remedy, the price is still "temporary" relief. We have in effect traded — in permanent relief for the so-called instant benefit, thereby abandoning our inherent right to a pursuit for health and happiness. In desire for more pain lies its removal.

This metaphysical paradox goes against the grain of contemporary popular culture. Undoubtedly it will be some time before it is understood much less accepted by those who refuse to let go of their illusionary lifestyle.

However, the Age of Aquarius will pressure those whose life pursuits are for momentary pleasure into an astonishing realization that the good life of permanency is theirs for the asking. A clear understanding of our cosmos will dictate that happiness, energy and peace o mind operate in a similar fashion as the light bulb. The more the desire of the negative pole, the greater is the necessity for the filament to restrict this fulfillment. For only then is the reality of circuitry achieved.

Take for example the common toothache. At the onset of pain, we have be programmed to immediately begin pill or aspirin — popping thus seeking and acquiring temporary relief. And when the pain returns to popping again.

How does the Kabbalist react to a toothache. At the first onset of pain, he is overjoyed by this unique opportunity to restrict the demand of that negative (pole), illusionary physical body for instant relief and fulfillment. He knows the benefit of pain; its cleansing and therapeutic cures for some of his Tikune. The soul, our 99% of reality becomes ecstatic with fulfillment as she observes a depressed and devastated corporeal body (who only represents 1% of our reality).

This is precisely the objective of the filament. Rejects the demands of the negative pole in the bulb for fulfillment of electrical current. The result! Circuitry.

Who does, in essence, feel pain if not our 1% corporeal body. She demands energy to erase the " lack of a physical well — being. Essentially pain is the warning signal that our free — flowing energy system has been disrupted. However, if we were to react to this free-universal demand of things — for — nothing without restriction, we shall inevitably suffer the consequences of the poor light bulb. When the filament permits the negative pole to make her simple demands for electric current and Mr. Filament is either asleep or non-functional, a short circuit develops

What seems to emerge from our insights into reality is that there are two opposite ways to deal with pain. The Kabbalist, while awaiting professional assistance to remove the pain, is in the interim enjoying his illusionary misfortune. Who knows, he may never require medical attention in as much as he may have restored his system to a circuitry of energy by his art of restriction. To restore temporary physical, relief is an illusionary corporeal entity of the 1%.

The usual toothache sufferer, meanwhile, is frantic and suffering, pill-popping until relief arrives. Then who knows what may be in wait for him.

So taking the path of least resistance may not necessarily

result in the betterment of our physical and mental well — being. Maybe the Kabbalist knows something we do not.

We each have a pool of knowledge from which to draw recollections of past indiscretions. Luckily, for most of us, those reminders of sojourns away from the straight and narrow are enough to keep us on our chosen paths. It is the man who resists the negative side of his nature who is to be commended and who will be blessed with the addition of new light into his circle. Instead of choosing the line of least resistance, the quick fix, instant gratification, the kabbalist chooses the line of most resistance, for it is resistance against the forces of darkness through the process of Binding by Striking, that brings Illumination to this world.

PRESSURE

Since the earliest days of civilization we have been under pressure — psychological pressure, pressure to perform at peak efficiency, pressure to live up to the expectations of others. Humanity has always had to fight for survival. We have always had to struggle to make ends meet. Fourteen pounds of air pressure per square inch has been pressing down on us since the dawn of time. Gravity has always created a burden which we have had to bear. Yet never before has the pressure been so great as it is today. Now, more than at any other time in history we have stretched the thin thread of our existence to the breaking point. We have come, it seems, almost to the end of our evolutionary rope.

The world is verging on a precipice of ecological disaster. Pollution and nuclear proliferation threaten the survival of every living thing on this earth. Rape, murder, terrorism — crime is on the rise. No longer can we travel in safety, no longer is it safe to walk the streets. Violent images come at us in a constant barrage — pushing us to the limits of emotional and psychological endurance. Stress, tension, urgency — the heat is on. This pressure cooker we call Malkhut is about to explode.

Why now, of all times, is this happening?

The Light, the *Or En Sof*, is the pressure we feel. It is telling us to realign our values to be in keeping with the new age. Now, in this Age of Aquarius, Malkhut is under more pressure than ever before. The times demand a new social dynamic if humanity is to keep pace with technology. The greed of this phase of our evolution, the waste and rampant materialism scream out for an outpouring of spiritual energy of equal or greater magnitude if balance is to be restored. From this day onward no peace will come to us, no tranquility — there will be no rest until the Light has been revealed.

No longer can we close our eyes to the Light of Creation. The Light is pressing in, instilling us with a sense of urgency, exhorting us on to greater and greater heights of consciousness, impelling us toward planetary consciousness. Now, more than ever, the Light of Creation demands revealment. There is only one way to relieve the pressure: Reveal the Light.

DIVERSITY OF PHASE

We take pride in our differences. We preserve and cherish them. We celebrate them, and commemorate them, and drown them in sorrow. We keep different customs, different habits and beliefs. We practice different religions and speak different languages.

Our body types are different as the colors of our skin. We have personal differences, differences on principle, different political systems and philosophies in which to express our differences of opinion.

Men die defending their differences, cities fall, empires crumble. So great are differences and so myriad that it would seem that they are insurmountable. Even in our wildest flights of fantasy it is hardly possible to conceive of a world without differences. And if there were to be such a world what a boring place it would be.

We love our differences. We thrive on them. They are our joy, our hope, our one salvation. Vive la difference!

There are differences between us to be sure, but comparatively speaking they are minuscule. Consider that the space between the particles in an atom is proportionately greater than the space between• the earth and the sun, and add to this the further consideration that the human body is made up of one percent matter — the rest is space and atoms. And of that one percent, the vast majority — perhaps ninety-nine percent — is comprised of the exact same chemicals and elements that go into making every other person.

So the next time you hear someone say, "the difference between you and me..." remember that the grand sum total of the differences between one human being and another amounts to one-one-hundredth of one percent. And the next time words become heated or push comes to shove, think about the one-one-hundredth of one percent in which we differ and the ninety-nine and ninety-nine one hundredths percent in which we are the same.

28

BRAINSTORM

A FLASH, A BRAINSTORM WAKES US FROM A sound sleep. Suddenly some idea or aspect of our lives comes into perfect focus. We are everything; the whole picture is clear. Then the Curtain sets in and begins to cloud our perception and we must hurriedly create mental connections in hope of retaining something of the essence of the inspiration. Sometimes we are able to grasp a fair portion of the flash's essence, while other times we are lucky if we retain even a pale recollection of what only seconds ago was an absolute certainty.

How can something that is an absolute certainty one moment be a pale recollection the next?

Flashes are expressions of the Infinite, glimpses into our own unique and complete fulfillment which we carry with us from birth through death and beyond. They are gifts, and like gifts of any kind they can be fully appreciated only by those who are deserving of them. The flashes that remain with us are ones for which we have restricted and thus alleviated Bread of Shame. When we are not prepared to accept the gift of a flash from the Infinite an illusionary installation of the lower seven creates a situation in which the flash of Light is said to be "drawn" below, meaning that is has come under the influence of the Curtain.

THE FILAMENT

In our discussion of the filament of a light bulb we learned that the negative pole and not the positive initiates any and all circuits of energy. The Line makes contact with the Circle thereby creating the circular condition necessary for the Light's revealment. The resulting circuit satisfies both the desire of the Line, to receive, as well as that of the Circles which is to share.

The brightness of a light bulb is determined solely by the size of the filament, not by the current that runs through the wiring system. The current is the same no matter what appliance is plugged into it, whether it is an air conditioner, the demands of which are great, or a five watt bulb, the desire of which is small. In a similar manner as a light bulb produces only that amount of light which its filament is capable of generating, so too can we manifest only that exact amount of Light which our filament (our capacity for restriction) allows our inner Encircling Vessels to reveal.

ILLUSION

From the kabbalistic perspective, that which is Infinite and eternal is real and that which is finite, including this world and all that is a part of it, is illusion. Our Encircling Vessels are of an Infinite nature, timeless and eternal; our bodies, conversely, are finite and therefore said to be of the illusion. Bodies come and go, but that which is real, the Infinite Encircling vessels within us carry on into Infinity.

How can Man, liar, thief, rapist, murderer, pillager and plunderer, in any way be deemed perfect?

Caught up as we are in outward appearances and the worldly struggle for survival it is difficult to imagine, much less embrace any concept contending that man, in spite of his myriad flaws, faults and infirmities, is at his core an expression of primal perfection.

The Tsimtsum created a space or vacuum between our illusionary (finite) physical aspect and our real Circular (Infinite) nature. That space, the gap, the illusion caused by the Curtain in the lower seven, conceals the perfection of our existence. When we, the emanated, said no to the endless beneficence of the Light we chose a situation in which a Curtain would forever remain between the illusionary aspect (Body) and the real aspect (Soul). From that moment on it became incumbent upon us to consciously bridge the gap of illusion called the Curtain through the act of restriction, thus earning the Light's blessing while at the same time removing our own Bread of Shame.

Our bodies, these Lines of limitation, along with this world of resistance and revealment, provide us with a set of circumstances by which we can amend, so to speak, our finite constitutions. The physical and mental ailments and conditions from which we suffer are aspects of the Curtain — obstacles, it is true — but also opportunities for correction and karmic adjustment. The real aspect of ourselves, the eternal aspect, though concealed, is perfect in every detail.

The rest is an illusion.

NEGATIVE SPACE

Earlier we learned that the ten sefirot of the Crown of Keter encircle (cause) only the Head or First Three (sefirot) of the Crown of the Line. The Curtain, located directly beneath Binah, the third sefira of the Line, divides the lower seven from the upper three thus preventing the Crown of Circles, which is of an Infinite nature, from melding with the lower seven sefirot which are finite. The Curtain and its inherent Desire to Receive is fully active in the lower seven but not in the upper three. This creates a situation whereby there is a space or gap in each of the Circular Sefira.

Many students, when this point is introduced, ask how is it possible that our inner Encircling vessels, which are said to be an Infinite expression of our primal perfection, can be flawed by the presence of a negative space?

The negative space found in the Encircling Sefirot is not a flaw within the sefirot themselves, but rather an aspect of the Line alone. The gap in the Line which is filled by the Curtain is firmly installed in the lower seven of the Line, but not in the First Three. The situation created when the Line connects with the Circle is such that the space or gap in the Line is transferred to the Encircling Sefirot. This situation creates a condition in which there is the illusion of a space or gap in each and every Circular Sefira to the extent that the Line transposes the negative space into the Encircling Vessels.

KLIPPOT

The word "sin" is derived from the concept of passing over. To sin is to intentionally overlook that which we know is right in favor of that which we know to be wrong. *Klippot* is a product solely of the linear aspect of Creation, the Line, and has nothing whatever to do with the circular aspect, the all-embracing Light. There is no evil, no duplicity in the Light of Creation — there never was nor will there ever be.

On this point Kabbalah differs from many other spiritual teachings in that it does not acknowledge evil as a separate force of existence, but rather as an aspect of Desire which stems from a deliberate disregard for the Light of Creation.

The Zohar expresses the view that the illusionary space separating the Emanator from that which He emanated creates a condition whereby *klippot* or evil can manifest, but the Light, whose only purpose is to impart joy and endless abundance, had not the slightest intention of allowing Its Infinite beneficence to be transferred to anything other than the original purpose for which It was intended, namely, the restoration of Light to the Encircling Vessels.

The Energy-Intelligence known as *klippot*, the evil "husks" or "shells" that permeate this phase of existence, are really conceal-ments or "passings-over" of Light. When the Creator withdrew to give free reign to our desire to alleviate Bread of Shame, a gap or vacuum was created between Itself and that which It had emanated. This negative space allowed for the entrance of *klippot*, a product of the Vessel's premeditated abuse of the Infinite life-force of Creation.

Klippot (evil) is a misappropriated vessel where there is no aspect of Desire to Share, a black hole that knows only an all consuming Desire to Receive for Itself Alone. The Light has but one harmless intention which is to reinstate Illumination to the Encircling Vessels, but the receiving Vessel, *Klippot* captures the Light and thus prevents It from fulfilling Its Infinite purpose. *Klippot*, then, becomes a negative force, animated by the Vessel's (man's) active and obdurate passing over of that which he knows to be the truth.

SPACE

Confusion sometimes accompanies the introduction of the following concept for it contradicts every known scientific, philosophical and mathematical construct and stands firmly opposed to all that is normally perceived to be logic and common sense: Space, the separation between people, mental, emotional and physical, the distance between objects, even the seemingly endless void between stars and planets, are all illusions. According to Kabbalah, there is no limitation of any kind in the real world, no time, no space, no friction or gravity, only the eternal presence of the *Or En Sof*. Space, then, from the kabbalistic perspective is an apparition, albeit a necessary one, still an illusion none the less.

A previous chapter advanced the kabbalistic axiom that

the Sefirot of Circles, being of an Infinite nature, possess no phase of the Curtain — other than the illusionary space which is transferred to the Circles through the lower seven of the Line. The illusion of space in our Encircling Vessels has nothing to do with the Infinite Light itself. The First Three sefirot on the Curtain's Light side experience no diminishment of the Light's endless abundance. The Line imposes limitation on the Circle, but only from the perspective of that which is on the dark side of the Curtain.

Only the First Three of the Line resemble entirely and have total affinity for all ten Circular Sefirot which comprise our Infinite primal energy-intelligence. Hence, the First Three sefirot of the Line are said to be "encircled" (caused) by all ten sefirot of the Circles, while the lower seven are said to be "drawn below" into the shadow of the Curtain. Unhampered, as they are, by the phase of the Curtain which encumbers the lower seven, the First Three or Head of the Line are in complete accord with all ten of the Encircling Sefirot and thus capable of instantaneous communication with the all embracing Circular aspect of existence.

The Encircling Vessels have Infinite ability and potential for revealment, but as their Illumination is restored through the finite straight vessels, they too give the illusion of being flawed by the identical deficiency, the space, that is displayed by the Line. Hence, between the last phase of the Crown of Circles and the first phase of the Wisdom of Circles, and so on through the ten subdivisions, we find an empty space or vacuum which though illusionary in terms of the our Infinite aspect, is all too real with respect to the human condition as it exists in his fourth phase.

Hence, our Circular, Infinite selves have potential to be in

constant instantaneous communication with all phases of the universal life force, while the lower seven, however, our physical presence, falls under the influence of the Curtain which is firmly
installed beneath the Head of the Line. This space in the lower
seven prevents us from experiencing our true unified relationship
with the world and the cosmos and prohibits us from penetrating
the vast body of metaphysical knowledge that lies hidden beneath
the negative trappings of finite existence.

We are comprised of infinite variations on this theme of
ten sefirot with the lower seven having no affinity for the upper
three. So while we find that the true, the real, the Infinite aspect
of humanity has potential to merge with the Circle, travel through
space-time, engage in telepathy and astral projection, and even
visit past incarnations, the lower seven which is separated from the
Infinite First Three have no such potential unless and until Bread
of Shame is relieved through an act of restriction.

Being separated from a good friend or loved one is an
intensely traumatic experience for some while for others it can be
nothing more than a mere inconvenience. After a year's separation
some couples return to the company of a seeming stranger, while
others pick up the tempo of their relationship, so to speak, without losing a beat. The difference does not necessarily have to do
with varying degrees of affection. The kabbalistic interpretation of
this phenomenon is that those who feel the greater sense of loss
are those for whom the Curtain has greater influence.

When we asked for a method by which to absolve Bread of
Shame, we took upon ourselves the responsibility of revealing the
Light. Only by creating the illusion of separation between the

Emanator and that which He had emanated was it possible to retain the illusion of separateness necessary for the emanated, to relieve Bread of Shame by re-initiating the connection with the Light.

Through restriction we can narrow the gap in the lower seven and thus lessen the mental, and emotional space between ourselves and others, and because the *Or En Sof* knows no separation or boundaries, it is possible for our Infinite Encircling vessels, which are a part of the Endless, to merge with the Infinite Light of Creation and thus traverse infinite light years of illusionary space in a single instantaneous leap of consciousness.

The illusionary space between the First Three and the lower seven in the Line causes not only personal alienation, but also the separation we feel with regard to the earth and the cosmos. Kabbalistically speaking, the Light is eternal, all pervading, never changing, while separation, space, and distance, being of a temporal nature, in that they change according to how they are perceived, are said to be illusions. In the real world, the *En Sof*, there is no room for negative space, separation being a characteristic only of the World of Illusion.

The illusion of space was inherited by our Encircling Vessels to give us the opportunity of absolving Bread of Shame by revealing the Light through restriction. Our ability to restore this Endless Illumination depends entirely on the extent to which we can transcend the limitation, the space, the illusion of negativity which is the Curtain.

Kabbalah provides us with a method by which to reconnect the seven of the Line with the ten of the Circle. The Line is the channel by which to restore Light into our Circular vessels. Through a regimen of well-tempered resistance we narrow the space between the finite and the Infinite, in effect squeezing out the space between ourselves and the Endless nature of the universe.

This restrictive action, known to Kabbalah as "purification of the Curtain" is the method by which the Curtain's influence is made less dense and hence the burden of its negative influence is nullified. The student of Kabbalah should be aware, however, that because the Curtain reasserts itself continually those who seek to lessen its darkening influence must act with equal diligence in revealment of the Light, for that is the method by which the illusion of space between our finite and Infinite aspects is reduced, making it possible to merge with the Circle of Creation.

TRANSFERENCE

Now it should be understood that because the Line feeds the Circle, so to speak, (the Circle remains in a state of unrevealment until it is acted upon by the Line), it is a reasonable and accurate assumption that the negative space, the Curtain, which is an inherent aspect of the Line, should be transferred to the Circle. Therefore, because the space in the Line is transposed to the Encircling Vessels, the Circles (Encircling Vessels) appear to have the same negative space as the Line, when in actuality they are "defective" only to the extent that the Line is incapable of restoring their full Illumination.

The Light of the Encircling vessels cannot be fully restored to its former brilliance through the limited creative process of the Line. The Light being of an Infinite nature, can never be completely fulfilled by that which is finite. Still, all of the Illumination received by the Encircling Vessels must manifest as a result of the action of the Line, which is why our Encircling Vessels appear to have the same linear deficiency as the sefirot of the Line when, in fact, they themselves are perfect. The only reason they appear to be flawed is that they inherited the space, along with its negative influence, the Curtain, from the Line.

CIRCUITS

Gravity, Earth's primal motivating force, provides ample evidence that the essential Energy-Intelligence of this the fourth phase, Malkhut, is the Desire to Receive for Oneself Alone. The great universal Energy-Intelligence, the Creator, conversely, has but one aspiration and that is to share. At first glance these two aspects of desire might appear to be in opposition, but closer observation reveals that actually this universal duality serves the balanced best interests of both phases of existence, for the separation of these two "opposing" forces prevents this fourth phase from reverting back to the unified condition extant before Tsimtsum.

The fusion of these two seemingly opposite aspects is called a circuit, and whether we are speaking of the poles of a battery, or those in a filament, or of the revealment of the Circular Light of Creation, this circular condition must be met in every instance where energy is manifested.

Actually, it is somewhat of an error to say that opposites attract. The opposition between these seemingly opposing natural forces is, like everything of this world, an illusion. The universal

Energy-Intelligence is circular — from a circle It was born and to a circle It will one day return. Thus, there being no opposition inherent in the Emanator, no space, no vacuum, and hence no opportunity for Desire to Receive (negativity) to enter, the attraction of opposites, though readily evident on this phase of existence, may be said to represent an artificial and hence illusionary condition in that the circuit is only temporarily disconnected.

The *En Sof*, endless Energy-Intelligence of the universe, is eternal, beyond even the space-time continuum, and therefore that which is temporary — including the attraction of opposites — is said to be illusion.

In fact opposites do attract, but only in the physical world which is itself an illusion. In the real world, the changeless, Circular world of the *Or En Sof*, opposites do not exist. Here in this fourth phase one may point to the positive and negative poles of a magnet as proof that opposites indeed do attract, however when one allows the two magnets to connect with each other, thus creating a circuit or circular condition, like magic the magnetic polarities disappear.

The reason for this, from a kabbalistic perspective, is that once the circuit is complete the true, universal condition becomes re-established. Each aspect of desire needs the other to complete its own unique fulfillment. Neither phase of the seeming dichotomy can rest until it is once again connected with its counterpart; neither can truly be consummated until it is once again mingling as an undifferentiated aspect of the unified force of which it is an aspect.

The kabbalist's firm conviction that fulfillment always precedes desire leads him to many conclusions that stand contrary to so-called logic, scientific precepts and "rational" thinking. He has accepted that the true nature of the universe is Circular and that therefore any and all separations, all expressions of finitude must be illusionary. Further, he reasons that as no space existed and therefore no room for negativity in the *En Sof* before the Thought of Creation there must be no space or separation in this world either, other than that which is illusionary, for the only difference between before and after the Tsimtsum, then and now, is that the Restriction created a condition in which the Vessel would no longer be aware of its connection with the Light. So we find that nothing whatever changed after the Restriction other than the Vessel's perspective of events.

The Tsimtsum, in other words, for reasons well established, made us blind to the true Circular condition of the universe, but the Restriction did not alter in the least the timeless, spaceless nature of the Light of Creation, but merely our finite, hence flawed, perceptions of It. The completed circuit was the original universal condition before Tsimtsum, and therefore the same condition must exist today, for as has often been repeated, the Light never changes. It is eternal, timeless, and perfectly still.

How can the Light, which is Infinite, suddenly become finite?

The answer is it cannot. The Light still shines in all its Infinite glory — the only difference being that the illusion of separation, the Curtain, inherent in this fourth phase, makes us blind to Its Endless majesty. Therefore, the kabbalist concludes that Circular fulfillment must be included in all aspects of the seeming universal dichotomy and that the accepted edict that opposites attract is, on the universal level, really an illusion. In other words, the circuit is complete.

Still, however well this revelation may serve the kabbalist in terms of his or her conceptual perception of reality, it does little in and of itself to dispel the problems and difficulties of the life of fragmentation which we finite beings must continue to lead. Hence, though it is true that the universal condition is Circular, we, as finite beings, must still cope with our linear existence.

When the Emanator withdrew He created the illusion of a vacuum, a gap, a space where none had existed before. That negative space, the Curtain, which allows us the opportunity of restricting voluntarily and thereby reestablishing a circuit of energy and absolving Bread of Shame, is destined to remain an integral part of this illusionary fourth phase of creation until such time as the great circuit of existence is again re-established as a unified whole.

The kabbalist seeks to operate on a conscious level of restriction so as to always have affinity with the Light. This is what is meant by a Circular Concept. By creating a circuit of energy he or she establishes, through Binding by Striking, a circuit of energy which not only serves the Light's purpose which is to share, but reveals his or her own unique fulfillment as well. Thus does the kabbalist achieve affinity with the Light of the Endless.

By completing the circuit we complete ourselves.

29

IF THERE IS A GOD...

KABBALAH PROVIDES AN ANSWER FOR THE frequently reiterated question as to why, if there is a Creator, does He allow so many bad things to happen?

The Energy-Intelligence of the Universe has nothing whatever to do with the negativity that permeates this fourth layer of cosmic experience. It was not the Creator's intention to allow negativity to rule the world. The purpose of Creation was to provide an opportunity for those whom the Creator had emanated to earn the Light's blessing by lifting Bread of Shame. This was the reason for the Creator's withdrawal and subsequent restriction.

In the *En Sof* before the Thought of Creation the existence of negativity was an impossibility. As was pointed out in a previous chapter, any Desire to Receive that might have manifested would have been instantly satiated. When we, the emanated, requested an element of free will sufficient to allow us to reveal the Light or not as we so desire, the Creator, who aspires only to share, was compelled to restrict Itself (Tsimtsum) in order to give expression to our desire to become individuated.

The Light's restriction, known to science as the Big Bang, created the fragmented situation in which we, as finite beings, find ourselves, and henceforth, from that moment on, it became incumbent upon humanity, the emanated vessels, to continually reestablish the connection with the Light through the limited creative process called the Line.

Desire to Receive for Oneself Alone, evil, *klippot* — all expressions of negative space — are energy-intelligences, born not from the Creator, but from the metaphysical "distance" that was, of necessity, placed between the Light and the Vessel to differentiate between them.

As with everything connected to this fourth phase, even this is an illusion. The Creator did not disappear. The Supreme Being is everywhere, without us and within us, permeating every phase and facet, every cosmic speck in the universe. Nor is the Creator any less willing to impart Infinite majesty to any and all who would care to pay homage to the original act of Creation which was Restriction. The only difference between the present universal state and the condition that prevailed before Tsimtsum is that we, the emanated, can no longer perceive with our five senses the Endless Presence without first relieving Bread of Shame.

Hence it may be said that *klippot* (evil) is the price we pay for our separate identities.

INITIATIVE

Unlike Tsimtsum which is totally resolute, the Curtain represents a flexible form of restriction. Like a window curtain, it allows more light into the given space, or less, depending on the degree of resistance with which it is confronted — a small gust of wind, for instance, will open it only a little way, a larger gust still further, whereas the hand of a person might pull back the curtains completely, allowing light to stream unobstructed into the room. In similar manner as one opens curtains with an extended hand, so too can the Curtains of negativity which surround everything on this fourth phase, Malkhut, be opened through metaphysical linear restriction, an act of will.

The Curtain is active below the Head or First Three of the Line. Between the Head or First Three sefirot: Keter (Crown), Hochmah (Wisdom), and Binah (Intelligence), and the lower seven sefirot: Hesed (Mercy), Gevurah (Judgment), Tiferet (Endurance), Netzah (Victory), Hod (Majesty), Yesod (Foundation) and Malkhut (Kingdom), there is a negative space or vacuum in which no Light can manifest. That dark gap is filled by the Curtain.

It was the contention of the Ari, Rabbi Isaac Luria, that the true nature of existence is unified, timeless, and perfectly still. What the kabbalist means when he or she tells us that this world is illusion is that the Circular aspect of existence is Infinite, but all aspects of worldly existence, having a beginning, middle, and end, are finite and therefore imperfect. Hence anything that is not an aspect of the Circular nature of existence is said to be illusion, including the Line and all of its myriad implications.

The need of the emanated to absolve Bread of Shame compelled the Emanator to restrict Its Infinite power so that the vessel's wish could be granted. Of course the Creator did not have to grant the wish of that which He had emanated, but to not do so would have precluded all possibility of the Light's revealment. As we know the Light has only one aspiration, to share, which is an impossibility without a receiving vessel.

This inalienable and eternal right of first refusal granted us by the Emanator is only a blessing for those who have mastered the art of resistance and restriction. Those who fail to exercise the option of restriction place themselves at risk of being inundated by the Curtain's negative influence, for they allow the Curtain to arbitrarily choose when, where, and how much Light the vessels will or will not receive; whereas those who restrict voluntarily have control over the power of the Curtain and are virtually impervious to its negativity.

In any event, it is Infinitely more rewarding to take the initiative of restriction. Through restriction we reveal the Light and we also reveal ourselves. Though it is never the kabbalist's intention of using Light for anything other than unselfish ends, still he or she walks always on a well lighted path.

THE LOWER SEVEN

It is said that the lower seven of the Line are greatly inferior to the Head or First Three. This concept seems to conflict with an earlier teaching that all of the sefirot are identical. The reason for this is that the inferiority or impurification referred to has nothing whatever to do with the vessels themselves, but to the quality of light contained within them. The lower seven, being on the dark side of the Curtain, are capable of revealing far less Illumination than those on the Light side and are therefore deemed to be inferior.

The Ari further taught us that the lower seven sefirot of the Line are inferior even to the lower seven of the Circles. Again by examining the two types of vessels, relative to the Curtain and the degree of Illumination which each is capable of manifesting, we can ascertain that Rabbi Luria, of blessed memory, was referring to the lesser revealment of which the lower seven of the Line is capable of producing. The lower seven of the Line reveal far less Light than the lower seven of the Circles for the simple reason that the Curtain is active in the lower seven of the Line, whereas the lower seven of the Circles are devoid of that liability. Thus, the lower seven of the Encircling Vessels are deemed superior to the seven of the Line.

We live in the lower seven of the Line. The Curtain is firmly installed above the lower seven in the fourth phase, Malkhut, creating a void between ourselves and our fulfillment. It is for this reason that our bodies have so much difficulty communicating with our minds and our minds with our souls.

We are not in touch with ourselves because the seven sefirot of the Line have no affinity with the ten Encircling vessels. There is only one method by which to bridge the gap, thus circumventing the Curtain and restoring affinity with the Light, and that is by effectively nullifying the Desire to Receive for Oneself Alone a condition which can only be brought about through an act of restriction.

ONE STEP BEYOND

To get caught up in the physical illusion is to cheat oneself out of the better part of life. Like talking without listening, eating without tasting, like reading the words in a book without making any attempt to understand the meaning, to accept only what is presented to us on the physical level is negate reality in favor of the illusion.

Because our physical aspect is destined to struggle for survival in the world of the seven denser sefirot does not mean that we have to accept this linear physical world as the be all and end all the existence. We contain, after all, an aspect of Infinity. The better part of us is continually connected with the Infinite Energy-Intelligence of the cosmos. The fact that our five senses are not aware of this cosmic connection is of consequence only in terms of our limited perceptions - it has nothing to do with the Infinite picture, the grand scheme of things. By seeing our actions within the context of the great universal network we create affinity with the Circle of Creation.

Does a hammer pound in a nail, or is it the mind?

The kabbalist will tell you that the mind pounds in the nail. The hammer and nails are mere material manifestations of that which was first perceived, undertaken, and completed on a metaphysical (thought) level. All that happens on a physical level has its roots in the metaphysical. Every effect has a metaphysical cause. If one accepts only the physical aspect of any endeavor, for instance if one sees oneself as only a nail pounder, is it any wonder that he or she will feel bored and unfulfilled? If, on the other hand, one sees his or her actions as channels, bridges between thoughts and finished products or manifestations, he or she will experience a sense of satisfaction at being an essential element in a circuit of fulfillment.

We are what we think. If it were possible to deal only with the physical aspect of existence, which fortunately it is not, life would be a one dimensional and utterly boring grind. By traversing the negative space between ourselves and our true Circular nature we reveal Light. Through resistance we bridge that gap — in effect squeezing out the negativity that fills the empty spaces. Thus do we complete the circuit of our own fulfillment and come to the realization that the real world is one step beyond.

THE SPARKPLUG

Consider from a kabbalistic perspective the spark plug:

The spark plug is a device used to introduce the spark directly into the cylinder of a gas engine. Notice the gap between the positive and negative poles. Take note also of the linear dimension of the spark plug and the vaguely humanoid form. Energy, the spark, must traverse that space to complete the circuit. Care is taken to calibrate the width of the gap to the distance which is most conducive to the spark plug's efficient operation.

The spark plug is designed for Binding by Striking on a rapid-fire schedule. As you will recall, a circular condition is always required for the revealment of energy. When, for any reason, the spark plug is unable to complete the circuit no connection is made and hence no energy can be revealed. When the poles become worn, for instance, the space increases to such an extent that the spark is unable to leap the gap. Another problem that can impede the performance of the spark plug is corrosion which causes a situation whereby sparks can no longer be initiated. When either of these conditions is allowed to persist the spark plug and hence the entire machine fails to operate.

THE FUTURE

Man's rampage against Nature seems all but complete. A massive, concerted, worldwide effort would have to be undertaken immediately if imminent dangers to our physical existence were to be avoided. Billions of dollars would have to be spent to clean up the air, billions more to purify the water. Laws would have to be enacted to prevent giant multinational corporations from plundering land and sea. Alternatives to nuclear energy would have to be aggressively researched and developed. The problem of world hunger would have to alleviated. Measures to reduce the birthrate would have to be adopted by countries all over the world. And it would not suffice to relieve only one or two of these life-threatening situations — they must all be solved. Each is so tightly interwoven with the others that the mesh is like threads of the finest cloth.

A case in point: The rapid expansion of the world's population contributes largely to the problem of hunger. Hunger, in turn, is the sole cause of the annual annihilation by slash-and-burn agriculture of hundreds of thousands of acres of rain and cloud forests. Also known as jungles, rain forests support over sixty percent of Earth's plant and wildlife in addition to absorbing vast quantities of carbon dioxide and providing a significant share of the world's oxygen supply.

Ozone, a form of oxygen, comprises a thin protective layer of the atmosphere which filters the sun's harmful infra-red and ultra-violet rays. A serious depletion of the ozone layer, as will occur with the decimation of the rain forests, will cause a condition of global overheating known as the Greenhouse Effect which will complete the destruction of the rain forests and ultimately sound the death knell for the human race.

It has been predicted that the rain forests, those life-giving natural wonders, those precious storehouses of untold knowledge, will virtually disappear as early as the year 2000.

The full consequences of man's undeclared war against nature are already being felt throughout the world. Each day several more varieties of plant and animal life disappear from the face of the earth, some not yet named much less studied.

We will never know what possibilities these extinct species might have held in store, what medicines may have been distilled from them, what tastes or esthetic pleasures they could have provided.

Precious plant life is disappearing at an unprecedented rate and the wholesale slaughter of endangered animals continues unabated. Elephants butchered only for their tusks, whales pushed to the brink of extinction and beyond to provide a variety of products which can be produced better and cheaper using synthetic methods — the evidence of man's selfish destruction is incontrovertible. He has run out of excuses. Now, at last, he must pay the price for his myopia and greed.

The future is here today, in the air we breathe, the food we eat, the water we drink. Hardly a day goes by when we are not reminded of the dangers of acid rain, PCB's, and other unnatural pollutants. Everywhere we turn we are witness to man's inhumanity, stupidity, cruelty, and even genocide. At last we are beginning to understand what the indigenous cultures have known all along: That any serious wound to nature is a wound to ourselves. That the balance of nature is delicate and tenuous. That everyone and everything is interdependent.

Yet understanding is not enough. Now, before it is too late, we must take immediate steps to dress the wounds of the damage already done. The hunger of the Third World populations is our hunger, their pain is our pain, their fate is ultimately our own. Only a small minority of the world's population is capable of doing anything to alleviate the world's problems   the vast majority being locked in circumstances of raw, bone-of-need survival. No longer is it sufficient for we who live in the more affluent societies to hide behind our relative comfort. No longer can we close our eyes to the havoc we have been wrecking. No longer can we plunder the earth with apparent impunity. No longer can we choose to remain ignorant of the dangers we are facing.

There was a time in recent memory when if a man spoke out against technology he was condemned as either a religious fanatic or, even worse, as an enemy of Progress. Technology was our savior and it was almost a sacrilege to suggest otherwise. Proponents of nuclear energy claimed that by the nineteen-sixties we would be living a life of ease and comfort with robots and computers taking care of all of our "menial tasks" and daily chores. Sleek, clean, nuclear powered monorails would sweep us to our destinations. Nuclear energy, it was touted, would be ours in abundance, electrifying cities for a cost of pennies per day. Those bright, hopeful voices are silent now and their brazen dreams of a nuclear tomorrow have dissipated into a cloud of radioactive dust.

Perhaps now the voice of reason can be heard.

Each generation has a responsibility to preceding and sub-sequent generations. Our burden is perhaps of a greater than any our ancestors were forced to bear. Our duty is no less than to shed Light on our own ignorance so that future generations may have a world in which to live. Now, today, we must begin to look at over-population, world hunger, and ecology, from a global perspective.

Vast reserves of cosmic energy surround us, energy which so far outshines that produced by the splitting of atoms that the comparison is like holding a penlight up to the sun.

The potential energy of the *Or En Sof* is within us and all around us, but to release those vast reserves requires an act of restriction.

The initial step in creating any bridge of understanding is a conscious decision. Men of conscience have always struggled against the forces of darkness. Kabbalists understand that resistance, the conscious re-enactment of Tsimtsum and the Curtain, are ways by which to bridge that gap and re-illuminate the primal purpose of Man.

It is time to draw the Line.

QUESTIONS AND ANSWERS

WHAT IS THE SOURCE OF THE VESSELS OF THE CIRCLES?
The Endless.

WHAT IS MEANT BY RESIDUES OR IMPRESSIONS OF LIGHTS?
When the Light withdrew from the ten Circular Vessels there remained Residues or Impressions of Lights. This remaining illumination induces a longing in the Vessel that prevents it from resting or achieving stasis until it draws in all the Light it once possessed. The terms Crown, Wisdom, Intelligence, and Beauty are synonymous with the attributes of the remaining Residues or Impressions.

WHY ARE THE CIRCLES ONE WITHIN THE OTHER?
Each inner Circle is caused by the outer Circle adjacent to it.

WHAT IS THE ROOT OF ALL THE LIGHTS?
The Endless.

WHAT IS THE ROOT OF ALL THE VESSELS?
The Circles.
WHAT IS THE SOURCE OF THE RETURNING LIGHT?
The fourth phase, Kingdom.

WHY DO THE LIGHTS PRECEDE THE VESSELS?
Because the Lights first emerged in three phases, one beneath the other, and these three phases were not called Vessels until the forth phase was revealed — it alone being considered a Vessel.

WHY DOES INTELLIGENCE NOT PRECEDE WISDOM?
Fulfillment precedes desire or longing. The Light preceded the vessel. Because in the order of emanation, we find that the complete always precedes and causes the revelation of the incomplete. In this manner the levels devolve one from another, every lower level being inferior to the level above it, until the revelation of this world, the most degraded of all.

WHAT IS THE SOURCE OF THE POWER OF CONTROL IN THE WORLDS?
The Curtain.

WHERE IS THE CURTAIN DRAWN FROM?
It is descended from the first Restriction.

HOW MANY CAUSES PRECEDED THE CURTAIN?
Two: The Restriction, and the Coming of the Light.

WHAT IS THE SOURCE OF THE VESSELS OF STRAIGHTNESS?

The Circles. The Kingdom of the Circles drew the Line and by its power the Curtain was made.

FROM WHERE DO THE CIRCLES RECEIVE LIGHT?

From the Vessels of Straightness. They themselves are unable to draw from the Endless since they do not have a Curtain and the necessary impurity.

HOW DO THE CIRCLES RECEIVE LIGHT FROM ONE ANOTHER?

By the power of the Curtain which "impresses" them without taking along its impurity. These impressions are called Windows of the Circles.

WHY MUST THE CIRCLES RECEIVE LIGHT FROM STRAIGHTNESS?

Because the Circles do not possess the phase of Curtain.

WHAT ARE THE WINDOWS IN THE ROOF AND FLOOR OF EVERY CIRCLE?

Impressions in the Circles created by the impurity of the Curtain.

WHAT CAUSED THE CIRCLES TO BE ONE BELOW THE OTHER?

The Light of the Line.

WHY DO THE CIRCLES REQUIRE THAT THE LINE JOIN THEM TOGETHER?

There is no juncture between the Sefirot of Circles and therefore they require the Line to join them together. See Ten Luminous

Emanations 2, p. 163:89.

WHAT IS THE DIFFERENCE BETWEEN SEFIROT OF STRAIGHTNESS AND SEFIROT OF CIRCLES?
The phase of the Curtain which the Sefirot of Straightness have and the Sefirot of Circles do not.

WHY IS THE POWER OF RESTRICTION NOT SUFFICIENT AND THE CURTAIN ALSO NECESSARY?
The function of Restriction is permanent, preventing itself from drawing light.

WHAT ARE LIGHTS OF STRAIGHTNESS?
The Light of the Spirit. See Ten Luminous Emanations 2, p. 164:92.

WHAT IS THE DIFFERENCE BETWEEN STRAIGHT ILLU-MINATION AND CIRCLING ILLUMINATION?
Straight Illumination is direct and finite. Circling Illumination, having no Desire to Receive, is Infinite.

IN WHAT WAY ARE THE CIRCLES SUPERIOR TO STRAIGHTNESS?
The Vessels of Circles do not possess a Curtain and impurity.

IN WHAT WAY ARE THE SEFIROT OF STRAIGHTNESS SUPERIOR TO THOSE OF CIRCLES?
The Sefirot of Straightness influence the Circles by drawing Upper Light.

WHY IS EVERY EXTERIOR CIRCLE SUPERIOR TO THE

OTHERS MORE INTERIOR?
The outer Circles are said to be the cause of the inner and are therefore closer in form to the Endless. "Exterior" means "pure."

WHY DO THE INTERIOR VESSELS OF STRAIGHTNESS SURPASS THE OTHERS?
"Interior" mens "more impure" which implies greater longing. Therefore the amount of Light that is drawn is greater.

WHY IS THE WORLD OF MAKING (ACTION) EXTERI-OR TO ALL THE OTHER WORLDS?
The fourth phase does not possess impurity sufficient to draw the Upper Light — in this respect it is the purest of all worlds.
See Ten Luminous Emanations 2, p. 265:98.

WHAT CAUSED THE EMERGENCE OF THE CURTAIN?
The Upper Light, reaching and touching the fourth phase, caused the immediate revelation of the power of the Curtain.

WHEN WAS THE CURTAIN MADE?
When the Upper Light reached the fourth phase, so as to Spread out in it, the power of Restriction (Curtain) was awakened to stop and deflect it.

WHY DOES THE ASCENT OF THE CURTAIN DEPEND ON THE EXTENT OF IMPURITY IN THE FOURTH PHASE?
Because the Returning Light which is the Curtain is equal to the Light which its original longing or Desire to Receive caused to descend.

WHAT ARE THE VESSELS OF RECEIVAL IN THE LIGHT OF THE LINE?
Even though the light of the line has only 3 phases, its vessels of receival derive only from the power of the fourth phase. The fourth phase itself, however, does not receive light, the root course of paradox.

WHAT ARE THE TWO KINDS OF TEN SEFIROT IN EVERY EMANATION?
The Ten Sefirot of Straight Light and the Ten Sefirot of Returning Light.

WHY IS THE RETURNING LIGHT CONSIDERED A VESSEL OF RECEIVAL?
Returning Light, having been born as a result of the Curtain in the fourth phase, is a phase of a Vessel of Receival exactly like the fourth phase itself.

WHAT DETERMINES THE MAGNITUDE OF THE RETURN-ING LIGHT?
The amount of Light that would have come to the fourth phase had not the Curtain deflected it.

WHY IS KINGDOM DISTINGUISHED AS THE CROWN OF THE RETURNING LIGHT?
Kingdom is the source of all Ten Sefirot of Returning Light and is considered, therefore, the Crown of the Returning Light.

WHY DO THE CURTAIN AND IMPURITY ACT AS ONE?
The Returning Light is equal to the impurity or "drawing power" of the Curtain.

WHAT PURIFIES THE CURTAIN?
Surrounding Light.

WHY ARE THE SEFIROT OF THE CIRCLES IN THE PHASE OF LIFE?
Because the Circles are not influenced by the Upper Light but receive illumination from the Line, their Light is Female, or Light of Life. See Ten Luminous Emanations 2, p. 167:110.

WHY ARE THE SEFIROT OF STRAIGHTNESS IN THE PHASE OF SPIRIT?
Because the Vessels of Straightness have a Curtain and impurity they are able to draw Upper Light and influence other Sefirot. Light which influences is called Male Light or Light of Spirit.

WHAT IS THE ATTRIBUTE OF THE FIRST THREE SEFIROT OF STRAIGHTNESS?
The first three Sefirot are void of the impurity of the Curtain.

HOW DO THE SEFIROT OF STRAIGHTNESS STAND WITHIN THE CIRCLES?
The first three Sefirot of the Line, termed the head are surrounded and have an affinity with the ten circular Sefirot. See Ten Luminous Emanations, p. 168:113.

Kabbalistic Terminology

ABSOLUTE FARNESS — The condition resulting when a change of form is so great as to become an opposition of form.

ASCENT — Purification. The purer is higher, the impure (thicker) is lower.

BEGINNING OF EXTENSION — The Root of all extension of Light. Also called Crown.

BINDER — The Kingdom of an Upper Sefira becomes the Crown of a lower thus each Kingdom "binds" every upper Sefira with the one below.

BINDING — The enclosing of the 10 Sefirot of the Head in the 10 Sefirot of the Returning Light.

BINDING BY STRIKING — The action of the Curtain which repels the Light and hinders it from entering the fourth phase.

BOUNDARY — The Curtain at each level stretches out and makes a "Boundary."

CAUSE — That which brings about the revelation of a level.

CONCLUSION— The fourth phase.

CORPOREALITY — Anything perceived by the five senses.

CROWN — The purest of all levels. Keter.

CURTAIN — The power of future restriction (additional to that of the Tsimtsum) which prevents Light from entering the fourth phase.

DESCENT — Impurification. Descent from a level. Thickening.

DRAWN — The descent of Light brought about by the power of longing (impurity) in the Emanation is said to be "drawn" down.

EMERGENCE TO THE EXTERIOR — A change in the form of Spiritual Substance.

ENCIRCLING — That which brings about the revelation of a level is said to surround or encircle that level.

ERECT HEIGHT — When the Lights of the Head are clothed in the Vessel of the Head we speak of the Countenance as being of "erect height."

ESSENCE — The Light of Wisdom is the Essence and "life" of an Emanation.

FAR — An extensive change in form

FROM ABOVE TO BELOW — "Straight Light" extending in the Vessels from higher to lower (purer to impure) levels is described as descending "from above to below."

FROM BELOW TO ABOVE — "Returning Light" drawn in order of levels from lower to higher (impure to purer) is described as ascending "from below to above."

GROUND OR FLOOR — The Kingdom of each level or world is termed the ground or floor of that level or world.

HEAD — The three Sefirot of the Upper Light.

HEAD — The nine Sefirot of the Upper Light which extend by Binding by Striking on the Curtain of Kingdom.

ILLUMINATION FROM AFAR— Light which is unable to enter the

Sefirot but surrounds it from a distance.

INDIVIDUAL — Light clothed in the Sefira of the Crown.

INNER LIGHT— The Light inside each Sefira.

IN PASSING — Each Sefira contains two kinds of Light, the Light which is indigenous to it, and the Light which is left there when the Light of the Endless passes through it. The latter is said to remain there in "passing."

IMPURITY — A strong Desire to Receive. "Thickness."

INTELLIGENCE — Reflection on the ways of cause and effect in order to clarify the final result.

JUNCTURE— Equivalence of form between two Spiritual Substances.

KINGDOM — The last phase. The tenth and final sefira from Keter in which the greatest Desire to Receive is manifested and in which all correction takes place. Malkhut. The physical world.

LENGTH — The distance from the purest phase to the impurest phase.

LIFE— Light which is received from the next highest level and not from the Endless, is called Light of Life or Female Light.

LINE — The Light found in the Vessels of Straightness. Also denotes finitude.

LIVING — The Light of Wisdom.

MATERIAL — The impurity in the Countenance from the fourth phase of Desire. Analogous to physical matter.

NEAR — Closeness of one form to another.

NOT JOINED—Changes in forms causes them to be "not joined" to one another.

NULLIFIED — When two spiritual substances are equal in form they return to one substance, the smaller being "nullified" by the larger.

ONE WITHIN THE OTHER — An outer Circle is defined as the

cause of the Circle within it. One Within the Other points to a relationship of cause and effect.

OUTER — The purer part of each Vessel is distinguished as the "outer" which is illuminated by surrounding Light from afar.

PASSING — The Light that passes through the sefirot is called "passing" Light.

PIPE — Vessels of Straightness are termed "Pipes" since they draw and confine the Light within themselves as a pipe confines the water which passes through it.

PRIMORDIAL MAN — The first World. Also called a Single Line. The root of the phase of man in this world.

PURIFICATION OF THE CURTAIN — Purification of the impurity in the fourth phase brought about in direct proportion to the Desire to Receive.

RETURNING LIGHT — Light which is prevented from entering any world by the Curtain

ROOF — The Crown at each level: true for both Sefirot and Worlds.

SOUL — The Light clothed in the Vessel of Intelligence.

SPIRIT— The Light clothed in the Vessel of the Small Face.

Spiritual— Devoid of material attributes, place, time and shape.

STRAIGHT — The descent of the Upper Light to the impure Vessels of the fourth phase is described as being "straight". Compare the swift "straight" descent of a falling stone with the slow meandering descent of a falling feather. The Earth's gravity (Desire to Receive) exerts a more direct influence on the stone. In a similar manner do the Vessels of Straightness, whose longing is strong, cause Light to descend swiftly in a "Straight" line.

SURROUNDING LIGHT — The Light which surrounds each Sefira, the illumination of which is received from the *En Sof* "at a distance."

THE ENDLESS — The source of the Vessels of the Circles.

THE FIRST THREE — The first three Sefirot: Crown, Wisdom, and Intelligence. Also called the Head of the Countenance.

THE LARGE FACE — The Countenance of the Crown in the World of Emanation, its essence is the light of Wisdom.

THE PURPOSE OF ALL OF THIS — The fourth phase of the fourth phase.

THE SMALL FACE — Six Sefirot of the third phase whose essence is the Light of Mercy, containing illumination from Wisdom without its essence.

WATER OF LIGHT — Light which descends from its level.

WHEEL — The Sefirot of Circles.

WISDOM — Knowledge of the final ends of all aspects of reality.

Z' 'T, THE SEVEN LOWER SEFIROT — The seven Sefirot, Mercy, Judgment, Beauty, Lasting Endurance, Majesty, Foundation and Kingdom,comprising the Body of the Countenance.

INDEX

KABBALISTIC ILLUSTRATIONS